The Complete Kit to
Selling Your Own Home
Smart, Fast and for Top Dollar

Joseph P. DiBlasi
Attorney at Law

SPHINX® PUBLISHING
AN IMPRINT OF SOURCEBOOKS, INC.®
NAPERVILLE, ILLINOIS
www.SphinxLegal.com

First Edition, 2003

Published by: **Sphinx® Publishing, An Imprint of Sourcebooks, Inc.**®

Naperville Office
P.O. Box 4410
Naperville, Illinois 60567-4410
630-961-3900
Fax: 630-961-2168
www.sourcebooks.com
www.SphinxLegal.com

This publication is designed to provide accurate and authoritative information in regard to the subject matter covered. It is sold with the understanding that the publisher is not engaged in rendering legal, accounting, or other professional service. If legal advice or other expert assistance is required, the services of a competent professional person should be sought.

From a Declaration of Principles Jointly Adopted by a Committee of the
American Bar Association and a Committee of Publishers and Associations

This product is not a substitute for legal advice.

Disclaimer required by Texas statutes.

Library of Congress Cataloging-in-Publication Data
DiBlasi, Joseph P.
  The complete kit to selling your own home : smart, fast and for top dollar / by Joseph P. Diblasi.
       p. cm.
  Includes index.
  ISBN 1-57248-353-9 (alk. paper)
  1. Vendors and purchasers--United States--Popular works. I. Title.

KF665.Z9 D53 2003
346.7304'363--dc22

                                          2003022488

Printed and bound in the United States of America.
VHG Paperback — 10 9 8 7 6 5 4 3 2 1

Dedication

To Laura—
You inspire me, uplift me, and simply amaze me.
Sei un Mito!

and

To my new son Dario—
You have shown me that life truly is a miracle to be treasured.

Acknowledgements

I am grateful to several people for their assistance to me during this project.

First and foremost, I want to thank my wife, Laura, for her unyielding love and support. This book was written during the first six months after our son, Dario, was born. As a result, when not at the office, I was often typing away while she, by herself, constantly attended to him. She not only never complained, but also made sure that I was comfortable, happy, not hungry, and not too stressed. Laura, this book is largely due to your strength and sacrifices.

I also want to thank my family (including my family in Italy) and friends (you know who you are) who offered many words of encouragement and support, along with many of their personal experiences in selling their homes. I am very fortunate to have each of you in my life. Grazie per tutto!

I would like to thank and acknowledge Mark Harrington of Harrington Moving and Storage in Andover, Massachusetts for the valuable assistance and great suggestions he gave me for the moving section in Chapter 10.

Finally, I want to extend my sincere gratitude and appreciation to John Nelson of Private Properties Realty in North Reading, Massachusetts and Anthony Salerno of Re/Max Real Estate in Andover, Massachusetts. Both have been close personal friends and business colleagues for many years. When I informed them of the nature of the book that I was writing, they were both very supportive and gracious. Moreover, they each provided me with valuable insight from a real estate broker's perspective that has greatly assisted me in the writing of this book. In the last chapter of this book, I suggest that those sellers who ultimately are not able to sell their home by themselves find a broker who is a person first and salesperson second. There are no better examples of this ideal than John and Anthony.

Contents

Introduction

As an attorney, I spend a large amount of my time assisting clients in obtaining relief from conflict and confusion. The greatest satisfaction in my work is providing my clients counsel to help allow them to *prevent* facing any such obstacles. As a legal self-help author, I hopefully am able to help provide this guidance on a much larger scale and in much greater detail and focus. When requested by this book's publisher to write a book that would assist those seeking to sell their own homes, I was intrigued by the prospect of helping people with a process that is so commonly-encountered, so important, yet so misunderstood.

The topic of the book coincided with somewhat of a new trend I was witnessing. In my real estate practice, I have not seen so much interest on the part of homeowners looking to sell their homes themselves as I have in this past year or so. After doing some research, I was able to see that my personal observations of my local area are quite consistent with the national trend.

One reason why America is the greatest country in the world is because of the great choices we have. Americans seem to always insist on having choices in their lives. Individuals and companies prosper when they are able to provide alternative products, services, and methods that satisfy this need. This demand for more options has recently spilled over into the home sales sector. Homeowners now have the choice between using a conventional real estate agent and selling their own home by themselves.

In the first chapter of this book, some possible reasons for the advent of the *for sale by owner* phenomenon are considered and why more and more homeowners are choosing this option. The type of homeowners who may expect to have the best chance of success at selling their own homes are also explored.

Chapter 2 examines the need to consider, at the outset, your options for future housing prior to setting out with selling your home. After mentioning the need to avoid buying another home without first having found a buyer for your home, the chapter poses and evaluates the options one has when having to sell one home and then buy another.

Whereas Chapter 2 focuses on preparing yourself for the pending move and its implications, Chapter 3 begins by focusing on preparing your home so that it is *ready for the public*. Such matters as the best and most cost-effective ways to make improvements to the home are considered, as well as provide suggestions for making the home look newer, bigger, and cleaner. In the last sections of Chapter 3, the importance of retaining an attorney at this early stage so that he or she can be there for you throughout the entire process is discussed. The value that a real estate attorney can provide is examined. Specific recommendations for choosing and retaining a capable one are made.

Chapter 4 begins the journey into the very important area of marketing your home. Assigning the right price is the most critical aspect of your marketing plan. Analyzed in detail, are the formal, as well as informal approaches to determining your home's value. Next, the seller is able to provide prospective buyers with all of the home's critical information at a glance by compiling a *listing sheet*. The elements that comprise the listing sheet are carefully reviewed, and suggestions on how to prepare the sheet to make your home stand out are given. A sample listing sheet is included for illustrative purposes.

Chapter 5 is dedicated to the vital element of advertising. Professional real estate agencies often write very effective ads that entice buyers to want to find out more. In order to assist *by-owner sellers* to refine this skill, much attention is given to what to say in the ads, as well as how best to say it. The federal *Fair Housing Act* is reviewed and its effect on homes-for-sale advertising discussed. The chapter concludes with a detailed analysis of the most effective places to advertise, including lawn signs, newspapers, and the Internet, and makes suggestions for how to best utilize each.

Once a prospective buyer is lured with smart advertising, you need to make the sale upon their viewing of the home. Chapter 6 focuses on the art of showing your home to the prospective buyer, whether it be via an open house or a one-on-one tour. Where and how to advertise the open house and the very important steps the homeowner should take prior to the *showing* are reviewed.

The goal to showing your house is to help make a buyer fall in love with your home just as you did when you first saw it. The documents and items that you need to have on hand and give to your buyer to make the viewing process complete and professional are set out. Reviewed are some well-tested methods of how to conduct the actual home tour, what to say, and how to comply with disclosure laws.

Once an interested buyer comes forth and offers to buy your home, you need to negotiate the terms of the sale. Contracts for the sale of real estate must be in writing. Chapter 7 analyzes where these written contracts (*Purchase and Sale Agreements*) can be obtained and the critical components they must contain. Some time-tested advice as well as actual language that can be inserted in the agreement for your protection and advantage are provided. Further, some tips on how to best respond to some of the common provisions that buyers seek to insert in the agreements are examined. The chapter concludes with specifics on how to effectively execute the agreement.

Chapter 8 spotlights some scenarios that a seller may encounter after a buyer steps forward. It offers answers as how best to handle them and prepare for the closing. This chapter will help make you an informed seller so that you will know how to approach and deftly handle these matters.

Chapter 9 examines the home-selling process at the closing. The various documents that a seller will need to have for the closing are itemized and described. Next discussed is the closing itself and the two different types of closings: the attorney/conference table closing and the title company/escrow closing. In order that you have a better understanding of what you can expect to sign at the closing, each of the common documents are reviewed and their purposes revealed. Copies of a few of the actual documents are provided for illustrative purposes.

For those that occupy the homes that they sell and therefore must physically move, Chapter 10 probes the world of moving and storage. Expert-provided tips for how to make the moving experience less stressful and less costly are included. Also explored are your insurance options provided by the moving company to help you decide which option will work best for you.

Chapter 11 concludes the book with a special look at how to handle the *hard-to-sell* home. The reasons why homes may be difficult to sell are analyzed, and advice is offered for each of the homes that fall into one of these specific categories. If the reason your home does not sell in a timely fashion is not explained by one of the hard-to-sell categories, some additional solutions are presented. For those that want to revert back to the traditional selling process of using a real estate broker, a detailed plan for hiring a first-rate, full-commission broker is included.

It was my honor to be asked to write this book, and it was my pleasure to write it for you. I hope that it serves as a useful tool for you as you engage upon the adventurous journey of selling your own home.

Best Wishes,
Joseph P. DiBlasi

chapter one:
Why Sell By Owner?

Savvy homeowners across this country are increasingly choosing to sell their homes by themselves, without real estate agents. In 2001, the Real Estate Brokers' own national website, **www.Realtor.org**, estimated that 20% of homeowners sold their home without a broker. Today, that percentage is regarded by many industry watchers to be about 25%. Many of those same industry watchers believe that this number will be 30% by the year 2005, and one study (by Gomez, Inc., a Waltham, Massachusetts based Internet-research group) predicts that by 2005, this number will be 75%. A few trends have occurred simultaneously to set the stage for this *For Sale By Owner* phenomenon.

WE ARE A QUICK STUDY

As we evolve to better accept new ideas, our natural curiosity, in turn, prompts us to further investigate them. Instead of just knowing about the existence of a new subject area, we often choose to explore deeper. The Internet allows us to have more and better information at our fingertips than we had in our entire school's library. The easy access to new information coupled with our curiosity has yielded a *do-it-yourself* craze. We have become comfortable challenging ourselves to become adept with these once-unfamiliar areas. The pride achieved and the money saved by doing-it-yourself are powerful incentives.

It is this avant-garde attitude and personality that allows us to avail ourselves of the information in this book and elsewhere, and confidently and successfully market and sell our homes without a broker.

EXTINCTION OF THE MIDDLE-MAN

The World Wide Web changed business forever. One of the Internet's most drastic impacts stems from the often unguarded access to information it offers. Prior to this, many businesses were successful because of their expert ability to provide specialized information for a fee. Often, a travel agent was consulted so that the availability and rates of airline flights and hotel rooms could be compared. Now, in less time than it can take to drive to the local travel agency, a person can log on to his or her computer, compare the rates and availability of several airlines and hotels, see virtual tours of the hotel property, browse the restaurant's menu, get directions from the airport, and book the entire vacation. The travel agency business has been harshly impacted by the Internet with the ease at which information can be exchanged.

The real estate agency is predominantly in the same *information* industry. It publicizes the availability of a *home for sale* in hopes of attracting a prospective purchaser. Prior to the Internet, the public would be hard-pressed to learn of the availability, location, and details of a property *on-the-market* without contacting a real estate agency.

The Internet has ended the real estate agents' monopoly on this information. By simple virtue of its size, the Internet is a much more powerful tool than the *MLS (Multiple Listing Service)* system. A cursory search of websites providing real estate information by sellers selling by themselves yields almost 1.5 million results. (A review and evaluation of some of these websites is discussed in Chapter 5.) Within these sites, buyers are able to locate property in any city or town in the nation, learn about every needed detail, and contact the seller directly without any interference from the *middle-man-agent*. Lastly, and probably not least importantly, the house may be sold without paying an agent's commission, which brings us to the third trend fueling the *For Sale By Owner* growth.

Not so Much Off the Top

It is no secret that real estate prices across the nation have risen dramatically over the past few decades. For sellers, it is great news to know that their largest purchase will likely return them a profit when they sell. This is hardly the case with most other purchases such as automobiles, furniture, office equipment, and even things bought specifically as an investment, like mutual funds. In 1992, the average existing home in the United States sold for $103,700. In 2002, the average existing home sold for $158,300, an increase of 52.7% (or 4.8% per year). During that same time frame, a typical real estate agency's fee has remained at 5% to 6%. So in 1992, the agency that sold that average home earned a $5,703.50 commission, while in 2002, the agency made a $8,706.50 commission. This surge in real estate values has given real estate agents an almost double growth rate over the cost of living.

What has happened as a result of these huge potential profits is what always happens in a market economy. Many outsiders notice the large profits being made in the real estate agency industry and enter the industry. As a result, many more agencies and agents are now vying for the same business. While the potential number of sales per agent has been reduced because of the increased competition, this has not changed the increasingly higher fee that the seller must pay to have an agency sell his or her house.

At a recent closing that I attended, I got into a conversation with one of the real estate agents about how the real estate market was performing. She proudly told me that her office had just listed a luxury home for 1.8 million dollars and that it sold the very next day. After inquiry, she admitted that the agency virtually incurred no expenses in the marketing of the home. I then asked whether the office had volunteered to reduce the approximately $100,000 commission. She shook her head, smiled, and stated—*"Our office does not do that."*

Because broker's commissions are tied to the sales price, it is very possible that the broker can pocket more money from the sale of the home than the seller. This happened with one of the homes I purchased. It was during the mid-1990s. The seller had purchased the home in the late 1980s, when housing prices were at unprecedented highs. Over the next few years, the market value of the home dropped due to the slow economy. The couple who owned the home were in the process of becoming divorced and decided to sell. As a result of the mortgage and settlement costs, including the broker's several thousand-dollar commission, the sellers actually had to *pay* money to sell their home to me. Homeowners are beginning to take notice of the fee that they will have to pay to the agency and, consequently, are more and more often deciding to attempt to market the home by themselves.

BEST CANDIDATES FOR SELLING THEIR OWN HOMES

As discussed, certain factors have come together to cause the large growth of homeowners who sell their own homes. These factors have changed the world of home selling and apply universally to all homeowners. However, while selling your home can be attainable by all, for certain homeowners, it is particularly suitable and highly recommended. Therefore, we next turn to examine those categories of homeowners who, because of their circumstances, absolutely should attempt to sell their homes by themselves.

Those Not in a Hurry

Everyone who puts his or her house on the market does so with the intent of selling and moving to another home. No one with this intent wishes to prolong the selling process more than necessary. However, some homeowners, for one reason or another, have the *luxury of time.*

Some homeowners may want to test the market and agree to sell their home only if they obtain *the right price*. If they receive this price, then they will find another home; if not, they will take their home off the market.

Others may have a large window in which to sell their home. For example, homeowners who will be selling their home and moving into a home or condominium community that has yet to be constructed will have a least a few months before they need to sell.

Similarly, many individuals, including *empty nesters*, sell their homes and move into apartments to free up monies with which to enjoy their retirement. They often can move into an apartment without much advance notice, and therefore can begin the process only when they find a buyer for their home.

Other homeowners may have a vacation home into which they may move after they sell their home and while they search for the ideal new home. Those who sell their investment property and not their residence, also may have the luxury of time.

Homeowners in these various types of scenarios, because of having time on their side, will be better suited toward marketing their homes by themselves.

Those Close-to-Home

Selling your home will likely require showing it to several prospective buyers at various times of the day and days of the week. This will be challenging, especially if you work. For this reason, selling your own home is better suited for those who:

- ◆ are retired;
- ◆ work out of the home;
- ◆ work close to home with flexible jobs;
- ◆ have a spouse or other adult at home; or,
- ◆ have a nearby friend or relative who can assist.

If you do not fit into one of the above-mentioned ideal categories, don't despair. As a *by-owner seller*, you will be able to schedule all showings at a time that is convenient for both you and your prospective buyer. This is not always possible when a home is marketed by an agent. They often only provide a notice to the owner a few minutes before the showing. Many owners who work a distance away from their homes, nonetheless, are able to provide showings on evenings and weekends, and for many buyers, this suits them just fine.

Those on a Well-Traveled Road

Exposure is one of the most important keys for selling. For retail businesses, the busier the street it is on, the more customers it can expect. The same is true for homes on *well-traveled ways*.

This advantage of *high visibility* helps homes on well-traveled ways *attract much interest*. For the cost of a *for sale* sign on the front lawn, your home can be *advertised* to the dozens or hundreds of vehicles that pass by each day. As a result, it may receive more attention than the small and costly ad in the local newspaper. Those with homes in high-visibility areas—your inherent advantage allows you to be well-suited to sell your home by yourself.

Those in a Seller's Market

Every so often, a specific geographical region experiences certain conditions that cause it to be a *seller's market*. These conditions may include one or more of the following:

- ◆ shortage of homes for sale in the market (commonly described as *low inventory*);
- ◆ low mortgage loan interest rates;
- ◆ heightened demand for homes; and/or,
- ◆ rapidly increasing real estate values/good economy.

When one or more of these conditions exist, it is likely a seller's market. When this occurs, you will often hear of homeowners who are able to sell their homes after only a few days. Often, the homeowner will receive much interest from prospective buyers and may receive multiple offers. It also is common during a seller's market for sellers to receive offers *above the asking price*. During these periods, the chances of success for a *by-owner seller* are much greater.

Those Selling a Non-Unique Property

A clothing store sells more pairs of denim jeans than it does alligator-skin pants. While someone eventually will buy the alligator pants, the jeans greatly outsell them because more of the store's customers prefer the look and price of the jeans. The same result occurs with the sale of real estate. Uniquely-styled homes often take longer to sell than the more traditional home because there are more available buyers for the traditionally-styled home.

Unlike in other countries, we in America buy homes for an intended, *finite* period. As such, we purchase a home knowing that someday we will want to sell it. Therefore, despite an initial inclination toward desiring a unique home, like the house designed like a ship complete with porthole windows, we are mindful of its potential limited market when it would be our turn to sell. This awareness serves to hinder the demand and makes the marketing of unique properties more challenging.

•   •   •   •   •

The above categories merely highlight significant home-selling advantages that a seller could exploit and thereby save paying a commission to an agent. While, the seller who fits into one or more of the above categories is likely to succeed in selling his or her own home, it does not follow that if you do not fit into any of these categories that you should not try to sell your home yourself. If the categories do not apply in your case, you still will be able to apply the concepts and suggestions in this book. And always remember, you will never know if you could have succeeded unless you first try. If you do not have luck, you can always revert to selling your home with an agent.

chapter two:

Before the For Sale Sign Goes Up

Once you accept an offer on your home from a buyer, the closing will typically occur within 30 to 60 days. Because the process happens so fast, it is best to be ready for the sale of your home as well as your future after the sale—before you put the *For Sale* sign in the front lawn. This chapter examines how best to strategically plan your sale and move so as to cause as little disruption in your life as possible. The next chapter will explore some of the more active steps that you will need to take to get your home ready to market before the for sale sign goes up.

PLANNING THE SALE OF YOUR HOME

It is recommended that you find a buyer for your home and have it *under agreement* prior to making an offer to buy another. To do otherwise, would place you at risk of having to purchase your new home without being able to use any of the *equity* from your current home. This obviously results in your having to carry the expenses of two homes at the same time; two mortgages, two real estate tax bills, two sets of heating and utility bills, two insurance policy premiums, two landscaping and upkeep bills, etc.

However, even if you wisely place yours on the market first, there is still some significant thinking to be done and questions to be answered.

◆ Where are you going once you sell your home?

◆ What sort of time will you need to find your new home?

◆ If you cannot find the *right* home within that time, do you have a back-up plan?

◆ Can you rent short-term or move in with relatives?

◆ What about the storage of your furniture and possessions?

These and other related questions should be discussed and answered prior to placing your home on the market.

Most buyers will take about 30 to 60 days to purchase your home from the date of your acceptance of their offer. *Cash buyers* (those not needing a mortgage loan), may be able to complete the deal even quicker. For some, a quick turn-around is not a problem. You may not need to purchase another home upon selling yours especially if:

◆ you will be renting an apartment with a flexible commencement date;

◆ you are selling a rental property or second home;

◆ you are moving in with others; or,

◆ you already have purchased your new home and were carrying the expenses of two homes simultaneously.

BUYING A NEW HOME

The question, *Where are you going?* is easily answered; and the question, *What will you do if you cannot find another home in time?* is irrelevant. However, if you need to buy another home, you have to consider the following several possible scenarios.

Find Another Home in the Required Time

Quite likely, you may have to try to locate your new home and purchase it on or before the day that a buyer buys yours. If you are lucky, your buyer may be willing to increase this time from the normal 30 to 60 day period. In any case, you can be sure that having to locate and buy your new residence under such restrictive conditions can lead to much stress.

Negotiate a Flexible Closing Date

If you do not have a new home in which to move, you may request to sell your home to your buyer only if he or she agrees to a *delayed closing date*, such as 90 days out from your acceptance of the offer, rather than the more typical 45 days.

In addition, you may also request that the buyer agree to include a provision in the *Purchase and Sale Agreement* (see Chapter 7) whereby you can move up the closing date sooner upon your finding a new home. This allows you more time to locate the right house so that you are not rushed into making this important decision. It also simultaneously locks-in the buyer to buying your home. Further, if you do find the right home right away and no longer need to close so far in the future, you *unilaterally* may change the date on which you sell your home to your buyer by providing him or her with the requisite notice that your purchase and sales contract specifies.

Such flexibility on the buyer's part is rare, but does happen. Unsophisticated buyers who are not working with an attorney may agree to this arrangement. A buyer who is currently renting or who is living with family may yield this flexibility to the seller in order to beat out other prospective buyers and make the deal work. These buyers may only need to provide thirty days notice to their landlord or, in the case of those living with family, no notice at all. (Such flexibility probably will not be available during a buyer's markets, when buyers are few compared to the number of sellers.)

Negotiate a Purchase of a New Home Contingency

One safe way to proceed is to only accept your buyer's offer for your home *contingent* upon your finding a new home. With this contingency, if you do not find a new home by a specified date, then you need not continue with the sale of your home and the deal will be voided.

The actual event that needs to occur before you are required to sell your home may vary. It may be based simply upon your offer on another home being accepted or it may be contingent upon the actual occurrence of the closing on your purchase. In addition, the date by which the specific contingency needs to occur is variable. You can make the contingency only valid within a few days after you accept your buyer's offer, or the contingency can remain valid through the day before the closing on your sale is scheduled. (The further along you are in the buying process in which you may back out, the better it is for you and the more opposition you may expect to encounter from your buyer.)

As you might guess, buyers usually are not eager to include such a provision in the sales agreement. It places the risk of *your* finding a home on them. If you are unsuccessful, their plans are destroyed, whereas you maintain the status quo. Moreover, if your buyer was, in turn, selling his or her home to buy yours, then this contingency will likely affect that transaction as well. However, because real estate is so unique, in a buyer's mind, there may be no satisfactory substitute for the home they seek to purchase. Buyers who fall head over heals for a particular home may be willing to make such a concession to the seller. In addition, in a seller's market, the lack of houses on the market may better allow sellers to avail themselves of such terms.

Rent Back from Your Buyer

This option allows you to sell your home to your buyer and still stay in the comfort of it until you are able to move. It is somewhat commonly employed by sellers who are moving into a new house or housing complex that is under construction and an exact move-in date is not ascertainable. It works best with buyers who do not have to sell a house in order to buy and who are flexible with their move-in date.

Although the buyer may be flexible about when he or she moves in, their mortgage restrictions typically will require them to schedule their purchase before the interest rate their lender committed to on the loan expires (the *rate-lock expiration date*). Consequently, the buyer can satisfy the lender's restriction and still be flexible for you by agreeing to buy the home and have you continue to occupy it and pay a periodic *use and occupancy* fee until the agreed-upon move-out date. The standard mortgage requires the buyer to physically move into the home within 60 days of the closing, so most buyers will not agree to have you stay beyond this period.

As with the *purchase of a new home* contingency, most buyers will not be overly eager to grant you this courtesy. Having you live in *their* home while they pay the mortgage and hope that you leave when you promise understandably carries significant risk. However, buyers who desire your property will often be willing to accommodate you.

The *Indemnification Agreement to Remain in the Property* that would be executed identifies the parties' respective rights and obligations and eliminates most of the buyer's risk. This agreement will seek to resolve such issues as:

◆ what rate the seller will pay for use and occupancy;

◆ how long the seller may continue to reside in the home after the closing;

◆ who will be responsible for the utilities, taxes, and insurance during the period;

◆ whether the seller will pay a security deposit to protect the buyer if damages occur during the seller's occupancy; and,

◆ what the penalty will be if seller fails to move out when promised. (see Chapter 10.)

Move into Temporary Housing

If your buyer does not agree to one of the options listed above, and you are not able to locate a satisfactory home by the date for your sale, your only option will be to find temporary housing.

Home sellers in this position commonly put their possessions in storage and move into an apartment or with relatives on a short-term basis while they continue their search for a new home. This option works well for sellers who are building a new home or moving into a new condominium complex still under construction. In these cases, their exact move-in date is likely undeterminable, and this option provides the seller with the most time and flexibility.

This option also works well when in a seller's market, where high house values and prospective buyers outnumbering available houses for sale. Home sellers, in this scenario, can attempt to *time the market* by selling their home to take advantage of the favorable market conditions, and renting an apartment or staying with relatives until the conditions change to be more favorable for buyers.

SELLING TIPS

Refusing to sell your home as a result of not finding another in time, is not a viable option as you will be in *breach of contract.* This allows your buyer to go to court to force you to sell it to him or her and also probably results in your having to pay the costs the buyer incurred to go to court, including reasonable attorney's fees.

chapter three:

Getting Your Home Ready for the Marketplace

Preparing a home cosmetically for sale is truly common sense, but it needs to be mentioned. I often hear from clients who view properties and are immediately *turned off* as a result of certain conditions the seller could have rectified quickly and inexpensively. You cannot please everyone on the amenities and features your home has, but you should strive to take care of the *little things*. Buyers are looking for properties that are neat and have been well cared for.

START OUTSIDE

You never get a second chance to make a good first impression. You have heard this before, and it applies here. The first thing buyers notice when they come to view your property is the landscaping.

Landscaping

A nicely landscaped lawn can increase the value of your home, often allowing the homeowner to recover all of a landscaping investment. Depending on the costs incurred and the amount the home's sale price increased, you could in fact recover more than what was spent on landscaping.

Psychologically, when buyers see well-trimmed landscaping, they believe that the owner takes pride in the home and therefore the home has been well cared for and not abused. Consequently, they believe that there has been less wear and tear, and that, for them, as the new owners, there will be less maintenance needed down the road.

House Exterior

After the landscaping, the prospective buyer next sees the *exterior* of the home. Nothing does more for the exterior than a fresh new coat of paint. Although it can cost at least a couple of thousand of dollars, depending on the home's size, a new coat will add vibrancy. If a new coat is not needed or money is tight, consider touching up some of the faded areas and areas of greatest exposure to your prospective buyer such as the front door and trim and other entrance areas.

MOVE INSIDE

Walls have a tendency to show the most wear and tear inside a home. Because walls are by definition vertical and in direct eyesight of buyers viewing the home, your prospective buyer will readily notice such imperfections as childrens' (and adults') handprints, scuffmarks, divots, nail holes, and stickers in the children's areas. Just as well-kept landscaping causes the buyer to presume positive attributes about the rest of the home, banged-up walls will cause the buyer to presume the home has suffered from a lack of attention and that defects could materialize after his or her purchase.

Painting the Interior

Painting is an especially wise investment as you prepare to sell your home because it is a task a non-handy person can do well without too much effort. Despite their current popularity, resist the temptation to choose a loud and vibrant color for your paint. Soft off-whites and very light neutral colors will make your rooms appear larger and likely will match with your prospective buyer's furniture.

Professional Carpet Cleaning

Beyond painting, there are other small projects that will help you efficiently achieve the neat and clean look that is valued by buyers. Professionally clean all carpeting. Stains in carpets will only serve to remind a prospective buyer than this is a *used* house. Moreover, the buyer may be forced to assume that the stains will not come out and that new carpeting is needed, thereby diminishing the value of the home in his or her eyes. Professional carpet cleaning should remove most stains and will leave the room with a fresh and clean aroma.

Professional House Cleaner

In the bathroom and kitchen, regrout the tile and backsplash so that all crevices are pure white. Replace aged shower curtains and scrub the tub, or if necessary, have a new tub surface professionally installed. If you have a fireplace, clean it thoroughly and remove all soot. For under one hundred dollars for most homes, a professional house cleaner can come in and clean all the rooms and surfaces. Afterward, if you found the right person (be sure to obtain a personal reference), the house will sparkle and smell wonderful.

Remodeling

Larger remodeling projects, done merely for the purpose of increasing the value of the home for a sale, for the most part, are not practical. Ideally, you should undertake a remodeling project only if you can expect to stay in the house for a while and enjoy it before deciding to sell. However, some remodeling may be in order after careful consideration.

Best Investment

In the most recent annual *Cost vs. Value Report, Remodeling Magazine* found that for remodeling within a mid-range budget, the addition of another bathroom gave the best return on investment. For every dollar that was spent on the additional bathroom, an additional $0.94 was realized at the time of sale (a 94% return). After this in descending order came the remodeling of an existing bathroom (88% return); the addition of a master suite (75%); window replacements (74%); and the remodeling of the kitchen (67%). The magazine also analyzed the returns if the remodeling was done in an upscale fashion. In that case, the remodeling of a bathroom yielded the best return (91%) followed in descending order by a bathroom addition (81%), the remodeling of the kitchen (80%), and a tie between the addition of a master suite and window replacement (77% each).

Make the Worst Room the Best

When deciding on which remodeling project to undertake, in addition to considering the above cost vs. value results, consider turning the worst part of your home into, hopefully, the best. In many homes, there are one or two particular rooms that lag significantly behind the others. For example, in one home the kitchen may have been neglected for thirty years and in desperate need of updating, while in another home the kitchen and baths may be reasonably well appointed, but the living room is dark and gloomy with matted carpeting. In each instance, if these respective rooms are overhauled, thereby transferring them from the worst room in the home to the best (or at least the mostly newly remodeled), the overall appearance of the home is increased greater than if any other room were to be overhauled.

Working with Tradesmen

While remodeling should be enjoyed by the owner and not undertaken merely to help a sale, there is another reason why such projects should not be done on the eve of putting your home on the market. Unfortunately, it is common for disputes to occur between the tradesman and the homeowner. Often, the tradesman's work progress is not at the pace expected by the owner, causing the owner to terminate the contract in the middle of the job. Other times, as a result of *unforeseen obstacles* the tradesman's final bill is higher than the estimate. In other cases, the homeowner is not satisfied about the tradesman's finished product and holds back payment. Also, there is the case where the homeowner's taste is larger than his or her wallet and money runs out before the tradesman has completed the work. In any of these scenarios, a dispute will arise between the parties.

The law will allow the unpaid tradesman to file a *mechanic's lien* on the owner's home. The lien will be recorded at the applicable registry of deeds and will cause there to be an *encumbrance* on the owner's title, much like a mortgage. The typical mechanic's lien statute allows a tradesman to *perfect a lien* on the property for work done to the home within the last 90 or so days. Therefore, a well-timed mechanic's lien filing by your tradesman could jeopardize your sale, or at least delay it and/or cause you to have at least the value claimed due by the tradesman held back from the sale proceeds until the matter is resolved. This could be devastating if you were relying on the full proceeds of the sale to purchase your new home later that day.

TIME FOR A YARD SALE

Even after you have cleaned, repaired, and remodeled, your home still may not look quite right. Probably, it is because it is holding too much *stuff*. This is often true when you have lived in your home for several years. *Stuff* often accumulates and accumulates and makes a home feel and look very small and cluttered. This is certainly not a positive characteristic in the eyes of buyers. When buyers see lots of stuff stored in the basement, attic, closets, garage, front and back porches, and in the spare room, they are bound to consciously or sub-consciously think at least one of the following.

◆ This house is too small. Obviously, there is not enough room for storage, and we very well may be in the same condition if we were to live here.

◆ If the sellers are not good with organization, I wonder how well they have kept up with the home's maintenance.

◆ Will the buyers be able to remove all of this stuff, or will they try to leave some behind with the house for us to deal with.

◆ If they do try to move all of this stuff out, will they scratch or damage the walls and floors in the process?

If you and your home are *stuff collectors*, you need to do something about this *before* placing your home on the market. Hold a yard sale and try to liquidate some of these items.

Advertise your yard sale with self-made signs on the utility poles in your area. A joint yard sale with others in the neighborhood can turn into a fun social event and the chances of success will be greater. The money that you make from liquidating your unneeded property certainly will help to pay the expenses that you will incur in the advertising and sale of your home.

SELLING TIPS

As a general rule of thumb, if you have not worn it or used it in the past two years, then it is safe to say that you won't in the future either. This item needs to be included in the yard sale.

If after your yard sale you still have considerable items that make your home still look congested, you should move to *Plan B*. Prior to advertising the sale of your home, rent a *self-storage unit*. Self-storage facilities have sprung up all over this country in recent years as our storage needs continue to grow. The self-storage units are quite reasonable to rent. A 10' x 10' climate-controlled, self-storage unit will cost you about $100.00 per month. For the few months that you can expect to need this unit, it is definitely worth the expense and effort required so that your home can once again look spacious and airy.

WORKING WITH AN ATTORNEY

Having an attorney represent you when you buy or sell real estate is always a wise decision. When you sell a home without a real estate broker, an attorney is of even greater value. For sellers not using a broker, an attorney will have somewhat of a dual role and you should approach him or her for such *broker-oriented* matters as marketing suggestions and advice to better evaluate the offers.

Even though you do not have your home on the market yet, now is the time for you to find and locate an attorney. The longer in the process you wait to find an attorney to advise you, the greater the chance for pitfalls. At the earliest stages, your attorney will be able to:

◆ advise you of the current market conditions;

◆ inform you of the local and state laws with which you must comply prior to selling your home;

◆ help draft and/or review your marketing flyers to ensure that they do not leave you legally vulnerable;

◆ provide you with the state-specific *Offer form*, the *Purchase and Sale form*, and any other locally-required forms; and,

◆ anticipate any title problems so that you may get a head start on rectifying them.

Just as important as retaining an attorney early on, is the need to find the *right* attorney. Often times, if a seller is selling through a real estate broker and does not have an attorney, the real estate broker will suggest one or more local attorneys. This option is eliminated for the seller selling his or her own home. There are, however, equally good sources for references.

Personal Recommendations

As is true when you are looking for a different restaurant or to see a new movie, *personal recommendations* for an attorney are likely the most reliable. Start out by asking friends and neighbors, who recently have purchased or sold a home, whom they used. Their answers to the following questions will assist you in narrowing your choice for an attorney.

How was their overall experience?

A good attorney should be able to make the home selling (as well as buying) process smooth and understandable. It is relatively common to encounter obstacles in the home sale process. However, a skilled attorney will be able to foresee potential problems, identify them, and work to correct them before it is too late.

Did the attorney keep in touch with them by telephone, mail, or email so that they were adequately prepared for the closing?

An attorney's value is only as good as what he or she knows about your specific situation. Likewise, your success is, to a large extent, determined by how well the attorney advises you. *Good communication is vital.* The attorney should be available to consult with the seller from the outset and thoroughly interview him or her so that all relevant information is relayed. The seller, after the initial meeting with the attorney, should have a solid grasp on the *big picture* and understand the likely sequence and timing of the events that comprise the sale process. From that point, the attorney should create an atmosphere that encourages questions and communication from the client.

Good communication for attorneys representing home sellers not using a broker is even more critical. As opposed to the buyer who may have a real estate broker, an attorney, a mortgage representative, and his or her bank's attorney available for consultation, the *by-owner seller* will only have his or her attorney. Consequently, the attorney should have a reputation for being available to clients and for returning telephone calls. The most skilled attorney in the world will be of little use if he or she fails to respond to a client's questions and not return telephone calls.

What was the attorney's fee?

Consumers are always sensitive to price. In the case of sellers selling their home without a broker, however, the question of *price* places a distant third in importance behind how the fee is charged and what is included in the fee. For the majority of cases, the difference between the fees of an expensive and inexpensive attorney for the representation of a seller is only a few hundred dollars.

A typical attorney will charge a *flat rate* for the representation of a home seller. This means that the attorney will not bill you by the hour. Unlike the court litigation process, the sale of a home is a relatively predictable process. Therefore, as attorneys are able to assess the amount of work involved, they are able to offer the seller the convenience and assurance of a flat-rate fee. Unless the sale of your home requires the undertaking of complex legal issues, such as having to probate an estate or evict a tenant prior to being able to sell the home, you should hesitate to engage an attorney who wants to charge you by the hour.

The right attorney also will be able to offer you an option or two with regard to his or her services. It is common for an attorney to have one flat rate fee if you want representation from *start to finish*, including the attorney's attendance at the closing itself, and another lower flat rate if the attorney represents the seller but does not attend the closing. Attorneys commonly also quote a flat rate fee for solely reviewing the purchase agreement.

It is also common for attorneys to charge a higher, flat-rate fee when they represent home sellers not using a broker. This is necessary because of the extra services they will provide, including drafting the *purchase agreement*, holding the deposits as the *escrow agent*, and evaluating the *offers* of prospective buyers.

Hiring an Attorney

If you are not able to obtain a recommendation for an attorney from a neighbor or a local friend or relative, there are other resources to consider. A skilled and respected attorney will be known by various departments at the town or city hall for which your home is located, especially if it is a smaller town. The staff in some of the offices there, including the tax collector's, assessor's, building inspector's, and planning departments commonly work with local real estate attorneys. They will have a good idea of the skill and reputation of some of the local attorneys. You also can call the state bar association and ask to be referred to a local real estate/conveyancing attorney. Finally, if you have the luxury of time, call a few of the attorneys in the local telephone book and make an appointment to meet a few of them. Your initial impression of them and the comfort level that they give you are often reliable forecasters.

Once you select an attorney, you will need to discuss his or her fee. While the typical attorney's fee for the complete representation of a seller is in the $500 to $1,000 range, an attorney will likely charge somewhat more when you are not using a broker. In relation to the value he or she will be providing, the price of the home you are selling, and the money you will be saving from foregoing the services of a real estate broker, the attorney's fee is a sound investment. There are, however, a couple of suggestions for obtaining a better deal and for ensuring high quality representation.

First, if you will be buying another home after your sale, make sure to let the attorney know this and inquire as to his or her price for representation on the purchase. Then ask if he or she offers a discount if he or she represents you *on both ends*—for the sale as well as the purchase. As you are presenting the attorney with two matters at once, you may find that he or she is willing to reduce the total fee.

Also, attorneys differ on when they request their fee be paid. With sellers, some attorneys request their fee at the outset while others will agree to be paid out of the sale proceeds of the house. If possible, refrain from paying all of the attorney's fee at the outset. (It is human nature for people to work more diligently to ensure their customer's satisfaction and hence their full compensation if there are monies due.)

It is best to retain your attorney before you even begin to market your home. At that meeting, be sure to inform the attorney that you wish to sell your home without using a real estate broker. As a result of their frequent contact with brokers, lenders, buyers, and sellers, most real estate attorneys will be in-tune with the current market conditions and can advise you of what you may expect. This insight may influence how you market your home.

For example, if the attorney informs you that it is a *seller's market* and that houses are typically selling fast and for asking price or more, you may want to price your home higher than what *you* believe to be *fair market value*.

Identifying Local and State Requirements

The attorney will also advise you of the local and state requirements for the sale of your home. There may be certain forms and disclosures that need to be prepared and given to prospective purchasers. There may be certain requirements that need to be met upon selling your home. For example, in Massachusetts, the seller must have their private septic system pass a strict inspection prior to closing. Meeting with your attorney prior to placing your home on the market ensures that you do not overlook any of these requirements and that you start off on the right foot.

Next, your attorney will need to draft and forward to you, the *purchase agreement form* that you can have available for prospective buyers. In some states, the purchase of a home is performed using an initial *Contract to Purchase* or sometimes referred to as the *Offer to Purchase*, and then a separate contract entitled the *Purchase and Sale Agreement*. In other states, the process is streamlined with the use of only the *Purchase and Sale Agreement*. Your attorney will be able to provide you with the correct versions so that the contract is readily available for any interested buyer.

Negotiating the Price

At your initial meeting, your may discuss with the attorney your preference that he or she also act as your *negotiator*. When a seller uses a real estate agent, prospective buyers present to and negotiate their offer for the home through the agent. Your attorney can substitute for the agent in this role.

Without someone else to receive the buyer's offer, the buyer must face and negotiate the purchase directly with the seller. This situation can be quite awkward. In the typical negotiation process, the prospective buyer will list a few *negatives* about the home to the broker—usually as support for making a less-than-asking-price offer. The prospective buyer will suggest that the seller should consider accepting this offer because of these negatives. The buyer is comfortable with this process because he or she can convey this message to the seller via the agent. The agent serves as an effective *buffer* and helps to reduce any offense taken by the seller.

If, on the other hand, there is no seller's agent, the interested buyer will need to negotiate directly with the seller. Understandably, he or she may feel uneasy directly telling the seller that this $500,000 home is worth only $450,000 because the kitchen and bathrooms are vintage 1970s, the carpets are soiled, and there are more weeds than blades of grass in the front lawn. In this situation, rather than making the $450,000 offer, the prospective buyer may decide against making any offer. You should speak to your attorney about his or her receiving all offers directly, so that you may inform all interested parties to deal through your attorney and not you.

chapter four:
Marketing Your Home

Now that you have selected and retained your attorney; and, evaluated your options should you not locate a new home by the time you sell yours, it is now time to commence the *marketing campaign*. The right marketing campaign will be the difference between locating a quick buyer and not selling your home by yourself.

DETERMINE YOUR PRICE

One common problem affecting *by-owner sellers* is their inability to objectively view their home and price it fairly. Many believe that their home is very unique or extra special and consequently attempt to sell it at an unreasonable price. People in the home-buying market are not impulsive buyers. They take much time, an average of 7-8 weeks according to **www.Realtor.org**, to compare an average of 10 homes before buying one. They are therefore somewhat sophisticated and will be able to sense when a home is overpriced.

A home that is overpriced will sit. A home that sits for a while will become *stale* and loose the appeal of being *new to the market*. Unlike new to the market or *just listed* homes, stale homes do not entice interested buyers to quickly make an offer before the home is snatched by someone else. Instead, with stale homes, the

SELLING TIPS

Pricing your home fairly and objectively will help to prevent your home from becoming stale.

perception with buyers is that they have plenty of time to compare other homes before seriously consider yours.

Similarly, I have encountered some people who have completely *undervalued* their home and sold it for much less than what they could have gotten using a broker. Typically, this occurs with elderly people who have not bought or sold a home in many years and who are not *in-tune* with the market. I recently had an older gentleman in my office whose wife had recently died. He was contemplating selling his home and told me that he thought he could get $200,000 for it. Being familiar with his town and his street, I was happy to advise him that he could sell it for nearly double that price.

Unless you are a keen observer of the local real estate market, you will not know the fair value of your home. Indeed, many professional real estate agents who use *comparison methods* to estimate the fair market value of a home are often *off* considerably and are surprised by the actual selling price. Real estate is not a commodity. It is, almost by definition, unique. Consequently, the comparison process only provides a very superficial basis for price estimation.

There are many characteristics of a home to compare, such as:

- age;
- style;
- size of house;
- size of lot;
- size of rooms;
- location within the town;
- location of the house on street;
- location of the house on the lot;
- exterior view;
- vicinity of services/conveniences;
- reputation of the town/city and school system;
- number of bedrooms;
- number of bathrooms;
- number of levels;
- quality of construction;
- reputation of the builder;
- condition of home;
- beauty of the landscaping;
- architectural layout;

- size of driveway;
- exterior of home;
- interior design;
- special interior features (such as central air conditioning and alarm system);
- special outside amenities (such as pool, sprinkler system, deck, and shed); and,
- topography of the lot (usable flat lot or steeply sloped).

Fair Market Value

Fair market value is defined as the price a willing buyer pays to a willing seller. The fair market value of your home is a function of many variables. Most of the characteristics of your home as set forth in the preceding section are variables that are *beyond your control*. For example, you cannot change the location of your home and land. Therefore, if the location of your home becomes more desirable (for example as a result of its vicinity to a development of newer and more expensive homes), with all else being unchanged, the value of your home will increase.

Some variables that affect your home's price are beyond your control but have little or nothing to do with your home. The condition of the local economy, the level of interest rates, and the amount of similar homes on the market are all good examples of this type of variable. If you are lucky to place your home for sale when there is a booming local economy, with low interest rates, and few homes for sale (in a *seller's market*), the value of your home will be considerably higher than if these variables were different.

The fair market value of your home also is a function of variables that are *not* beyond your control. The condition of the home and landscaping and the quality and quantity of your advertising and marketing campaign are the two principle variables over which you have almost total control. The prudent seller should look at all of these variables when considering the price to ask for the home. I have seen home-sellers, including those using brokers, underestimate the favorable seller's conditions or fail to make simple, cost-effective improvements and consequently forego significant money when they sold their homes.

Comparison Method

The most accepted manner for determining the fair market value for your home is the *comparison method*. In theory, the value for your home can be approximated by comparing your home and its features with other homes nearby that have sold recently. This method can be pursued in one of two ways, formally or less formally. To determine the fair market value formally, a licensed *real estate appraiser* is needed. A licensed real estate appraiser, as a result of training and certification, is the foremost authority on evaluating the value of real estate. You can expect to pay between $250 and $500 for a full appraisal. An effective way to locate a qualified and licensed real estate appraiser is to call the lending department of your local bank. Lending officers work closely with licensed appraisers and they will be able to provide you with a couple of names.

The appraiser will come to your home to inspect and evaluate it. He or she will make note of all of the aforementioned characteristics that make your home unique. Next, he or she will locate up to five similar homes in the area (usually in the same town and, if possible, in the same part of town) that have sold recently. Appraisers try to use homes that have sold within the last three or four months for comparison. Using older sales will compromise the integrity of the process, as the market conditions going back more than three or four months are likely different than they are at present. While an appraiser will make note of most, if not all, of the items in the list of how homes differ, the actual variables he or she uses for comparison will likely be:

- location of home;
- size of lot;
- exterior view;
- design and appeal;
- quality of construction;
- age;
- condition;
- gross living area;
- whether there is a full basement and whether it is finished;
- the condition, quality, and amenities of the utility systems;
- whether there is a garage;
- whether there is a porch, deck, patio or fireplace; and,
- outside features, such as pool, shed, and fence.

The appraiser will use a grid table to display the results. There will be one column for your home and one for each of the other homes used for comparison. The rows of the table are for the variables listed on the previous page.

(The following is an excerpt from the sales comparison table of an actual appraisal report.)

Item	Subject	Comp.#1	Comp. #2	Comp. #3
Sale price	?	384,500	395,000	374,500
Location	Average	Average	Average	Average
Size of Lot	50,500 s.f.	45,000 s.f.	28,300 s.f. (+12,000)	25,700 s.f (+12,000)
View	Average	Average	Average	Average
Design/Appeal	Colonial	Colonial	Colonial	Colonial
Quality of Const.	Average	Average	Average	Average
Age	Built 1985	1982	1986	1988
Condition	Average	Average	Average	Average
Gross Living Area	2,640	2,260 (+6,840)	3,060 (-7,560)	2,464 (+3,160)
Basement	Full, unfinished	Full, unfinished	Full, unfinished	Full, unfinished
Functional utility	Average	Average	Average	Average
Heating/Cooling	FHW/none	FHW/None	Both Central (-9000)	FHW/None
Garage/Carport	2 Car Blt. In	2 Car Blt. In.	2 Car Blt. In	2 Car Atch.
Porch, Patio, Deck Fireplace, etc.	Deck, Porch 1 Fireplace	Equal Porch 1 Fireplace	Equal Porch 1 Fireplace	Equal Porch 1 Fireplace
Fence, Pool etc.	None	None	None	None
Net. Adjust. Total		+6,840	-4,560	+15,168
Adj. Sale Price Of Comparable		$391,340	$390,440	$389,668

As you can see from the table, when the comparable home differs significantly from your home (the Subject) in a particular category, the appraiser uses a calculated dollar amount to approximate the value of the difference. For example, in the table above, the lot size of the subject home is 50,500 square feet. The Comparable Home #1 has a 45,000 square foot lot. In the appraiser's estimation, although there is a 5,500 square foot difference in area, this does not represent a significant difference and therefore no dollar adjustment is made. Comparable House #2, however, has a lot of 28,300 square feet, significantly smaller than the subject. Consequently, the appraiser calculates the 22,200 square foot difference to be worth $12,000.00. Comparable Home #3 has 25,700 square feet of land and, although being somewhat larger than Comparable Home #2, the appraiser also uses the same $12,000 figure to represent the difference in the value with the subject home's lot size.

The adjustments can also have a negative value. For example, with the *Gross Living Area* category, the Subject Home has 2,640 square feet of living space while Comparable Home #2 has 3,060 square feet. As a result of having 420 additional square feet in space, the Comparable Home #2 is given a negative value of $7,560.

When the comparable home fares better than your home in a particular category, a negative value is used for an adjustment. When the comparable home fares worse, a positive value is used. When all categories of the comparable homes have been compared to the subject home, all adjustments are totaled and added to the reported sale price of the comparable homes. The result is the *Adjusted Sales Price of the Comparable Home.* As a result of accounting for all significant differences between the subject home and the comparables, the adjusted sales price provides a scientific market value for your home. In our above example, the Subject house has a market value between $389,668 (adjusted sales price of Comparable House #3) and $391,340 (adjusted sales price of Comparable House #1).

Comparative Market Analysis

The less formal approach to determining your home's worth is to perform a *comparative market analysis* (CMA). This approach does not entail the thoroughness of the features/variables comparison or of the specific positive and negative dollar value adjustments seen in the appraisal. Rather, it is performed by reviewing the selling price of visually-comparable nearby homes and comparing the homes on a more basic and superficial level. As a consequence, the resulting value determined by a CMA is not a precise dollar figure, but instead, typically a range of value, such as $385,000 to $400,000. The CMA can be done, however, at little or no cost.

SELLING TIPS

Depending on the market conditions, the asking price and eventual selling price of homes can vary substantially. So, using the asking price of comparable homes is not a reliable method.

First you will need to locate the addresses of homes in your neighborhood that have sold within the past six months. Once you know the address of the home that recently sold, you should contact the assessor's office of the town or city hall and ask them for the name of the owner. (Chances are that, since it often takes months before their records are updated, they will provide you with the prior owner's name. However, regardless of whether they give you the name of the prior owner or the new owner, this name will aid you in your research). You next need to go to the applicable registry of deeds and review the *Deed* executed for each comparable home sold. The deed most likely will recite the price paid by the buyer. If not on the deed, the purchase price is often located on some other document available to the public, such as a *Transfer Declaration Page*, which is used in some areas.

Most registries have online access and, in these cases, you should be able to view copies of the deeds without leaving your home. Typically, the online procedure for retrieving and viewing deeds is quite user-friendly. Often, the user is able to find the deed knowing only the address of the property or the seller or buyer's name.

Internet Comparative Market Analysis
Now, with the growing sophistication and utility of the Internet, there are several sites that can provide you with accurate sales price information. Some sites will provide you with recent sales prices of all homes with the requested range of street numbers in case you are not sure of which homes have sold recently. Examples of worthy websites are:

www.fsboadvertisingservice.com/saleprices.asp
and
www.domania.com

Other websites will provide you a CMA of your home online after you input the requested information about your home. Some impressive national sites include:

◆ www.housevalues.com
◆ www.ourhomesprice.com
◆ www.homegain.com
◆ www.priceahomeonline.com

Most of these sites are tied to real estate broker agencies and will forward your name and contact information to a local broker who will urge you to allow them to list your home. If you do not mind the solicitation, then the free information obtained through these websites will be worth it. If you do not want to be contacted by a broker and do not mind paying for a CMA, then check out **www.ushomevalue.com.** This online service will provide you with a comprehensive CMA for your home as well as recent sales data for nearby comparable homes. You can expect to pay approximately $50.00 for their report.

Additional Consideration

Regardless of whether you use the formal or informal method of determining the value of your home, you should consider your own situation as well as some *intangible market conditions* to arrive at a final asking price. For example, if the appraisal dictates a selling price of $450,000, but you are a very patient seller not in a rush to sell, you are just coming into the prime spring buying market, and the interest rates are low, you may consider listing it at $460,000 or even $475,000. If, on the other hand, the CMA suggests a range of $440,000 to $460,000, the inventory of other homes for sale in your area is high and many are sitting for a while and you need to sell quickly, then you may want to list the home at $440,000 or lower. In other words, evaluate your own personal situation with the current market conditions to *tweak* the actual asking price for your home.

Finally, there is a bit of psychology behind effective home pricing. Although $399,900 is only $100 less than $400,000, the difference is much greater subconsciously. The first number in the price of the home is very powerful. A buyer may believe that a house in the 400s is out of his or her financial ability, but may be willing to stretch for a home at $399,900. Moreover, this same buyer may search for a home to buy on a for sale by owner website and limit his or her search by price and ask to see advertisements for homes from $300,00 to $400,000. If your home is priced one dollar more than the $400,000, or if the website provides results exclusive of the low and high limit ranges, the buyer will not see your ad.

DESIGN YOUR LISTING SHEET

Once you have arrived at your desired asking price, you will need to put together what is referred to as a *listing sheet* in anticipation of providing prospective buyers with needed information. A listing sheet is used widely by real estate brokers to convey the *nuts and bolts* of their customer's home to other brokers as well as to potential buyers. It is a one-page repository of all of the necessary factual information concerning the home. Although not legally required, *by-owner sellers* should create their own sheet because of its effectiveness, as well as the wide-spread expectation of buyers that each home for sale will have one. A sample listing sheet is produced on page 37.

A seller's listing sheet should be made available to potential buyers in a few different ways. It can be placed in the *sign box* beneath the *For Sale* stake sign placed on the side of the road in front of the home. It is typically handed to prospective buyers at open houses and it can be part of or the sole item of a direct-mailer.

As indicated earlier, buyers, on average, will purchase a home after viewing 10 homes during the course of 7 weeks. After visiting even a few homes in only one weekend, it is very difficult for the buyer to recall the various features of any one particular home. This recall difficulty makes the necessary comparison process among all of the viewed homes virtually impossible. The listing sheet resolves this problem. After a long day of home shopping, the buyer can sit down, lay out all of the listing sheets, and make an *apple for apple* comparison of the various homes. The listing sheet will refresh the prospective-buyer's memory as to the size, layout, condition, and features of each of the homes. It is at this point that the listing sheet proves its worth.

Photograph of Your Home

The listing sheet typically contains a prominently-placed photograph of the home. In addition to accurately depicting the exterior and landscaping of the home, the photo will help a prospective buyer to immediately recall your home after he or she has viewed several others. Take a reasonably, close-up photograph so the home nearly fills the dimensions of the frame. Angle your shooting perspective so as to capture attractive amenities, such as nice landscaping and flowers, and also so as to avoid any eyesores, such as low-hanging utility wires, cars parked on the street, or the neighbor's adjacent garage. Its always a plus to have a *picture-perfect* blue sky as a backdrop.

The photo also should reflect the current season. While a photo of a snow-covered roof and lawn might evoke warm and snuggly feelings for some, it will not for your prospective buyers in

SELLING TIPS

If your home does last over a season without selling, take an updated photo to keep it from looking stale.

July. Instead, they not-so-subtly will be reminded of how long your home has been for sale and will wonder if something is wrong with it.

Vital Statistics

In addition to the photo, the listing sheet should provide the vital statistics of the home, including: the price of the home, the type, size, and description of each of the rooms, a quick description of the home's features and mechanical systems, and some remarks to help highlight the qualities of the home. Also in the vital statistics section, be sure to provide:

- ◆ the style of the home (colonial, contemporary, townhouse-style condominium, etc.);
- ◆ the number of rooms;
- ◆ the year the house was built;
- ◆ the gross living area; and,
- ◆ the lot size.

For the number of rooms, do not count bathrooms or rooms below grade (a finished basement). For gross living area, multiply the dimensions of each separate foundation by the number of floors sitting above grade thereon. For example, a two-story Colonial with a foundation measuring 44 feet long and 28 feet wide, there is 44 x 28 x 2, or 2,464 square feet of living area.

Detached garages, basements, and attics are not counted for purposes of gross living area. The lot size can be reliably retrieved from a survey or from your deed—both of which were probably given to you when you purchased the home. Your local assessor's office at the town hall also will have this information. For condominiums, the lot size would be either *not applicable* or *common* as in owned in common with the other unit owners.

The remainder of the listing sheet is commonly broken down into sections labeled *Rooms*, *Structure*, *Appliances/Options*, *Services/Utilities*, *Legal*, and *Remarks*. Each section is analyzed below so you can both provide the information that your buyer seeks, as well as present your home professionally.

In the *Rooms* section, each room should be listed with its approximate dimensions. Underneath the *Structure* heading, list the color and material of the exterior, the type of roof, foundation, windows, and floors and whether or not certain structural amenities exist, such as a full basement, fireplace, pool, deck, shed, and porch. For the *Services* section, identify the type of heating system (e.g., natural gas), how the hot water is heated, the amperage for the electrical system, the presence of any air conditioning system or individual units, whether water is town supplied or private well, and whether the waste disposal system is town sewer or private septic or cesspool. In a section entitled *Appliances*, identify whether or not certain appliances exist and will remain with the home, and if so, their type. Be sure to comment on all appliances and options that complete your home, including:

◆ stove;

◆ dishwasher;

◆ microwave;

◆ disposal;

◆ refrigerator;

◆ trash compactor;

◆ air conditioning;

◆ washer;

◆ dryer;

◆ central vacuum;

◆ security system;

◆ smoke detection system;

◆ carbon monoxide detection system;

◆ lawn sprinkler system; and,

◆ outdoor lighting.

If you are not certain whether you want to take a certain appliance with you, list it as *negotiable*. The last category is commonly labeled *Financial* and *Legal*. Here, provide the assessed value of the home (from your recent tax bill), the zoning district (ask the assessor or building inspector's office), the book and page number for your deed at the registry of deeds, and, if a condominium, the monthly common area charge (assessments).

Condition

The *Remarks* section is the one section of the listing sheet where you can make your marketing skills shine. This is the place to reveal what exactly it is about your home that others would find most desirable and interesting. Generally, space on the one-page listing sheet only allows for a few descriptive sentences—so make them count. Focus on the two or three characteristics of your home that you believe make it special and want your buyer to know and remember. Chances are the things that you liked about the house when you bought it and still like now are the very things that your buyer will like.

Remember that buyers value clean and neat homes. If truthful, definitely mention its condition. Use descriptive words such as *mint, pristine, exceptional, meticulously-maintained,* or *move-in condition.* If you have undertaken some of the cosmetic and remodeling projects previously discussed, you will have a better chance to make this claim.

Location

The location of the home should be highlighted in the *Remarks* section wherever possible. Real estate is unique principally because its location is permanent. Accordingly, the value of any particular home will rise and fall based on its location.

Location can be interpreted in various ways. It can refer to the home's external view or proximity to a geographical point or part of nature, such as an ocean, lake, conservation land, hilltop, or a high floor in a high-rise condominium building. It can refer to the home's being in a particular neighborhood or part of town, such as—near the park, in the downtown shopping area, or close to the interstate.

Think about how the location of your home can be best portrayed and incorporate it in the *Remarks* section to your advantage. For example, if the home is located in a suburb of a major metropolitan area, then chances are your prospective buyer works in or near the city. In this case, mention its vicinity to commuting routes—*seconds to Route 24* or *two lefts from Highway 192.*

Qualities

After discussing condition and location, you can highlight qualities of the home itself. Three top qualities that homebuyers are known for valuing are:

◆ size of the bedrooms;
◆ size and features of the kitchen; and,
◆ closet/storage space.

If you can favorably refer to any or all of these, do so. Buyers like bedrooms that are at least large enough to comfortably accommodate their bedroom furniture and allow a little *moving around* room. If your bedrooms satisfy this test, be sure to inform your prospective buyer.

Kitchens are almost unanimously believed to be the most important room in the house come sale time. An old axiom says, *No matter where I serve my guests they like my kitchen best*. Just think about the gatherings and parties that you have hosted at your home and you likely will agree. The kitchen is the focal point for you and your family as well as for all your guests. Be sure to point out the highlights of your kitchen that will entice a buyer. Examples include:

◆ large eat-in kitchen;

◆ gourmet kitchen with Corian (or granite) countertops;

◆ bright and airy;

◆ center-island;

◆ ceramic-tiled;

◆ gleaming cabinets;

◆ with new appliances; or,

◆ lots of cabinet space.

The third house-related characteristic that buyers most value is closet and storage space. Americans are enamored with buying clothes, small appliances and electronics, sporting equipment, landscaping tools, and other items of personal property. In fact, it seems that our desire for these things is limited only by the size of our closets and basements. Having a place for everything and putting everything in its place accurately states our desire to have large and orderly storage space. Homebuyers want to feel comfortable that they will not be limited in their ability to acquire property because of a lack of space and that they will have room to expand. Accordingly, point out your closet and storage attributes using the generic phrase *lots of storage space* or such other specific descriptions like:

◆ master suite with walk-in closet and dressing area;

◆ full basement;

◆ double-door shed in back yard;

◆ built-in bookshelves; and,

◆ walk-up attic.

Special Features

A final category to consider when writing the *Remarks* section is your home's *special features*. Some features will distinguish your home by their mere mention. Examples include:

- ◆ an in-ground pool;
- ◆ hard wood floors throughout;
- ◆ a finished and/or walk-out basement;
- ◆ a brick fireplace;
- ◆ high (or cathedral) ceilings;
- ◆ new roof (heating system, windows, etc.);
- ◆ security system;
- ◆ central air;
- ◆ sunroom (or deck, patio, or porch);
- ◆ two-car garage;
- ◆ lawn irrigation system; and,
- ◆ wiring for DSL/surround-sound.

In mentioning these special features, don't feel bashful that you are heaping praise about your own house. It is the house, and not you, that is the object of the acclaim. Your pride will be respected and envied by a buyer.

Contact Information

The last item to include in the listing sheet is your contact information. Include your name, telephone numbers at which you prefer to receive calls, and a fax number (if you have one) so that interested parties can fax you an offer. Also, if you wish to have all offers go through a third party (your attorney), include his or her name and contact information as well as indicating:

Kindly refer all offers to [your attorney].

A sample *Listing Sheet* follows on the next page.

427 Maple Street, Pleasantville $489,900

Remarks: Year-round resort setting awaits you. Level backyard abutting a private pond. Classic center entrance Colonial in move-in condition. New great room with cathedral ceiling, 3 walls of glass, and wrap around deck. Corian counter kitchen, spacious rooms, and gleaming hardwood floors.

GENERAL INFORMATION		STRUCTURE		APPLIANCES/OPTIONS	
Style:	Colonial	Color:	Cream	Stove:	Thermadore
Lot Size:	1.3 acres	Exterior:	Cedar	Sink:	Single Corian
Approx. Sq. Ft	2700	Roof:	Asphalt	Disposal:	No
Age	15 years	Floors:	HW, tile, ww	Dishwasher:	Yes
Rooms	9	Fireplaces	1	Refrigerator:	Yes
Bedrooms	4	Basement	full	Microwave:	Yes
Baths	2.5	Laundry:	first floor	Trashmasher:	No
Garage	3 car	Deck:	yes	Air Cond:	No
		Porch:	no	Central Vac:	Yes
		Pool:	no	Security	No
APPROX. ROOM SIZES				Sprinkler Sys	Yes
Living Rm:	19 x 13				
Dining Rm:	14 x 13	SERVICES/UTILITIES		LEGAL/LISTING	
Family Rm:	24 x 13	Electric:	200 amp	Book	1826
Kitchen	13 x 24	Heat:	FHW	Page	187
Great Rm:	21 x 18	Fuel:	oil	Exclusions:	
Master BR:	13 x 20	Hot Water:	tank	Work bench in	
2nd BR:	12 x 16	Sump pump:	No	basement,	
3rd Br:	12 x 16	Zoning:	R1	Refrigerator, washer,	
4th Br:	12 x 8	Water:	Town	dryer	
		Sewer:	Private	Taxes:	$4,800
				Assess:	$375,000
				Schools:	Reagan
				Owner:	Hannity

Kindly refer all offers to [name and number]

chapter five:
Advertising

The price has been determined and the listing sheet has been polished and printed. Now all you need is to find some interested buyers. To do so, you must embark on a well-thought out advertising campaign to attract interest in the home. The campaign should resolve what will be said, where it will be said, and to whom it will be said.

DESCRIBING YOUR HOME

Advertising is important to give one product a better appeal in the marketplace. It is designed to help it stand out from its competitors. Often, advertising campaigns for consumer products do not focus on providing specific information about the actual product. Instead, they seek mostly to create brand awareness by using colors, logos, catch-phrases, sounds and music, stimulating visuals, and celebrity endorsements. Real estate is quite different.

With real estate, by definition, each property is different. A residence can only occupy one particular parcel of land, and that parcel of land, in and of itself, makes it unique. Even with condominiums and co-operatives, the location of the unit within the complex or within a building makes the property just as unique. Each of the several characteristics regarding price determination, such as age, size, and condition of the

SELLING TIPS

The more an advertisement for a home moves away from providing specific information, the greater is the risk that the reader will be disappointed.

home, only add to its uniqueness. Consequently, the advertising of homes, cannot be esoteric, and instead must be about providing specific information. The reader will subconsciously presume negative qualities when important information is not provided.

For an example, consider this actual recent advertisement for a home placed for sale (only proper names have been removed):

> *Water-front parcel overlooking the Cove with panoramic vistas of the Harbor and the ocean beyond. Direct access to a private beach. Desirable neighborhood within walking distance to all amenities including public bus service, beaches, shopping, and the world famous art colony. The center is within a five minute drive as is access to the highway.*

The writer of this advertisement focused just about 100% of the text on the location of the home. Although the location sounds very appealing, nothing was said about the home itself. In fact, even though it was an advertisement for a home, the exact same words could have been used if it was an advertisement for a buildable lot only.

After reading the advertisement, we do not know the condition of the home, the size of the home, the number of bedrooms or bathrooms, the style of the home, whether it has fireplaces, a pool, a two-car garage, a finished basement, central air conditioning, or hard wood floors. In fact, because it fails to include any specifics, the reader is left to think that while the location sounds nice, since the ad does not say anything else, the home itself must be in lousy condition and lacking in features and amenities. A question of whether the seller is trying to lure in a buyer with the location may well enter into a buyer's head.

For comparison purposes, lets look at a couple of other actual recent advertisements for homes offered for sale in the same publication as the one above.

> ◆ *Pristine 10 room, 3600 sq. ft. raised ranch, private 1 1/2 acre tree studded lot. Living room with fireplace, dining room, 4 bedrooms, 2 1/2 baths, kitchen, large family room with brick wall fireplace, laundry room, office, screened-in porch (16x24) and much more. 10 minutes to Rt. 1, 95 and 128. Excellent school system. Most desirable neighborhood. Great for children!*

◆ *Spacious colonial on beautiful wooded lot. Wonderful neighborhood. Perfect for entertaining. Bright kitchen with maple cabinets, eat-in kitchen adjacent to all-season heated sun room and family room with gas fireplace. Large master bedroom with jacuzzi and walk-in closet. Flawless hardwood floors in living, dining and family rooms. 10 minute drive to beaches. Owners have not had pets—no dander or pet damage.*

These advertisements, although using almost exactly the same number of words as the first ad, give a much fuller description of the home and property. They focus on the key important areas: size, condition, location, and features. By using such vivid words and phrases as *pristine, spacious, tree-studded, bright, flawless,* and *most-desirable,* the reader can visualize what is being described and also can sense the seller's pride. Both ads convey a sense of spaciousness as well as a clean and neat condition.

Word and Phrase Guide

As you begin to write the text for the advertisement for your home, look at other homes' ads. Decide if the words and phrases that you see fit well for your home. If you get stuck, refer to the *Word and Phrase Guide* below for some descriptive words and phrases that may be just what you are looking for.

CONDITION	LOT	ROOMS	LOCATION	MISC
pristine	oversized	generous	convenient	charming
move-in	manicured	spacious	borders on…	sprawling
sparkling	professionally	well-proportioned	water/mountain	perfect for
mint	landscaped	light & airy	-views	entertaining
better than new	tree-lined	bright/sunny	easy access to…	curb-appeal
well-maintained	corner-lot	plenty of	nestled on…	adorable
gleaming	mature	storage space	walk to bus/train	one-of-a-kind
updated	plantings	finished basement	private setting	opportunity
meticulous	room for	walk-in closet(s)	most-desirable	cozy
	expansion level	high/cathedral	(name) school	not a drive-by
	fenced-in	ceilings	district	finely-crafted
	back yard	open floor plan		

LEGALLY PROMOTING YOUR HOME

While getting your advertisement to sound right is a matter of art, using the right words is a matter of law. The *Fair Housing Act* (Title 42, United States Code, Section 3601 (42 U.S.C. Sec. 3601), a federal statute, prohibits many forms of discrimination in the marketing, sale, or rental of housing While some portions of the law exempt private owners who are selling their own home, the section regarding discrimination in advertisement explicitly exempts *no one.* Therefore, after you have drafted your advertisement, review this section to make sure that it does not violate the Fair Housing Act.

In simple English, the law states:

> *It is unlawful to in any way advertise the sale or rental of a residence that in some way or manner indicates a preference, limitation, or discrimination based on race, color, religion, sex, handicap, familial status, or national origin. It is also illegal to have an intention to so prefer, limit, or discriminate.*

Your Ad

In general, be wary of any words or phrases that might indicate a preference or discrimination based on any of the factors stated in the Fair Housing Act. And specifically:

◆ do not attempt to describe the make-up of the neighborhood. You can say *great neighbors* or *great neighborhood,* but you cannot say *Irish neighborhood, many Hispanic neighbors,* or *adult complex.* (Although widely used, it is not suggested that you use *exclusive* in describing the neighborhood as it may be argued that it has a connotation of excluding certain groups.) and/or

◆ refrain from making references to near-by landmarks that may indicate a preference or aversion for the protected groups. (For example, describing your home as being *down the street from the synagogue* or *walking distance to the Sons of Italy* would likely violate the Fair Housing Act.)

As an example of how tricky the Fair Housing Act can be, a lawsuit was brought in Portland, Oregon as a result of the *Remarks* section of a seller's listing sheet. It stated, *Adults only over 40.* Even though the listing was for a condominium in a complex that lawfully restricted residency to adults over 40, the party bringing the suit was able to convincingly argue that the phrase discriminates against families with children (because it seemingly prohibits or shows an aversion for children) and therefore violates the Fair Housing Act. Because of the vulnerability, the defendant believed it necessary to settle out of court.

Individual complainants who believe his or her rights are violated by the ad may take you to court under the Fair Housing Act. If the court decides that unlawful discrimination occurred, the home seller can be ordered:

- to compensate the complainant for actual damages, including humiliation, pain and suffering;
- to provide injunctive or other equitable relief, for example to make the housing available to the complainant;
- to pay the federal government a civil penalty to vindicate the public interest (maximum penalties are $10,000 for a first violation but up to $50,000 for a third violation within seven years); and,
- to pay reasonable attorney's fees and costs.

PUBLISHING YOUR ADVERTISEMENT

The more difficult task is not what to say about your home, but instead, where to say it. The best and most efficient placement of your advertisement calls for careful planning and strategy. There are hundreds of places to publish an advertisement, including newspapers, magazines, radio, broadcast television, cable television, the Internet, aerial signs, subway billboards, the inside cover of a matchbook....you get the idea. Ideally, it would be great to use each and every advertising option so as to inform the most number of people about your desire to sell your home. However, because advertising generally costs and because most is expensive, the idea is to place your ad in the medium or media that gives you the best value, or more colloquially, the *biggest bang for your buck*.

Lawn Sign

In the multitude of options for your advertising dollar, the lawn sign is the *no-brainer*. With a lawn sign, you have a captive audience. Each and every vehicle, jogger, and bicyclist who passes by your home will be a reader of your advertisement. Think about it for a second. When you drive, jog, or bike down a road and you come across a sign, whether it is a road sign, a broker's *For*

Sale sign, a yardsale sign, or a business' street sign, it is almost impossible to ignore. Your attention cannot help but be drawn to it.

A pre-printed *For Sale by Owner* sign can be purchased from most hardware stores. Typically, it is a red sign with white lettering and a white rectangular space left blank for the owner's telephone number. Unfortunately, these signs are not worth the $5.00 that they cost. Often, the signs are too small, not placed at the appropriate height level, and contain a telephone number that, because of the inadequate space or the poor choice of writing instrument, cannot be read by passers-by. Often, these signs are placed only a foot or so off the ground in a delicate metal frame. Because of their design and placement, they resemble a yardsale sign or the sign of a home repair contractor advertising while he or she works at a customer's home. For this reason, the typical, generic *For Sale by Owner* sign will be subconsciously viewed as a contractor's advertisement and not for the sale of a home.

For those who do actually recognize the sign for what it is, the generic, store-bought *For Sale by Owner* sign conveys a message to those who look at it that the owner is either not serious about selling the home and/or not very knowledgeable about the home selling process. The sign will not give a feeling of confidence that the matter will be handled properly.

Instead, make the investment in having a sign professionally designed and made. You can go to your local sign shop and describe what you need. There are also many websites of sign manufacturers that specialize in real estate and *For Sale By Owner* signs and accessories. Type in *for sale by owner signs* or *real estate signs* using your favorite search engine and you should retrieve dozens of choices.

The Sign

You need one main two-sided sign (for size, the standard real estate size is 20" x 30", but check with your local building inspector's office for size limitations). The sign should have large letters that say *For Sale By Owner* along with your pre-printed telephone number. In addition, it could contain a custom, couple-word phrase that will catch the attention of passers-by—*4 Bdrm-2.5 Bath—3,300 sq.ft—Finished Basement*, etc. It is not a good idea to print the asking price of the home on the sign as you do not want to eliminate any potentially-interested buyers without their having seen the home first.

If you use a *for sale by owner* advertising Internet service, print the website and/or identification number for your home. Many of these Internet advertising sites offer their own sign with their pre-printed information. These services are discussed in greater detail toward the end of this chapter.

The Post

A sign post that, once installed in the ground, will position your sign so that it is about eye height for those traveling in automobiles—about four feet off the ground. You may choose to go higher, but signs lower than eye level likely will be overlooked. Again, check with the building inspector for any height restrictions. The post can be a sleek metal design or a wooden T-post. The aforementioned websites offer these sign posts or you can make your own from lumber supplies bought at your local building supply store. In addition, the sign needs to be able to fasten to the post, usually with eyehook screws or loops. Finally, the post needs should be able to accommodate a smaller, ancillary sign called a *rider*. On a wooden T-post, the rider sign slides into a groove on top of the horizontal post.

The Rider Sign

A *rider sign's* purpose is to convey current information for the home's marketing. Publicizing the day and time of an *open house* is one good use for a rider. If you choose to create your own website for the marketing of the home, you can print the website address. It can also advertise that there has been a *price reduction* or one characteristic about the home that makes it special, such as *2 Acres*. For a consistently-polished look, you should have these riders professionally pre-printed with as many different messages as you like.

The Flyer Box

A well-done *For Sale* sign will hopefully grab the attention of the passers-by. If it does, the next thing that they will do will be to take a good look at the home itself. If the exterior of the home and the grounds initially appeal to them, they will have an immediate curiosity for more information about the home. That is where the *flyer box* comes in handy.

The flyer box should be either attached to the sign post or right at its base. It is a weather-proof, envelope-type container that will hold your *listing sheets*. The words *Take One* should be printed on the front of the box. The idea is to grab the buyer's attention with the sign, heighten that attention with a cursory viewing of the property and the exterior of the home, and pique his or her curiosity with the listing sheet. All this is done so that he or she then calls you to arrange a viewing of the home. A professional flyer box can be purchased via some of the aforementioned online companies, or you can make a do-it-yourself one.

The Directional Sign

Finally, and especially if you live on a quiet road off from the well-traveled roads, you could purchase a few pre-printed directional signs pointing passers-by to your *Home for Sale* or *Open House* with the address printed below. These signs are generally smaller in size and placed on more economical wire holders close to the ground. You will need at least one of these signs for each road between the main road and your road.

The major point to remember about your lawn sign is that it should not be amateurish but should project the professionalism with which you will exemplify throughout the selling process. You do not need to re-invent the wheel when constructing your sign. You can choose among the many *for sale by owner* signs and accessories available at sign stores and over the Internet. You should model the signs after the ones used by real estate agencies. A well-done lawn sign will cost you only about one hundred dollars or less. But, despite its low cost, it will provide unbelievable exposure, especially if you are on a well-traveled road. Nearly all of the people that pass by, live, or work in the area will become an instant local sales force who will mention your home whenever they speak to their friends and family desiring to move into a new home or into your neighborhood.

Newspapers

Newspapers are another very good advertising option. They are published very frequently, either daily or weekly, and the classified information they contain is very current. This is important to buyers who do not want to waste time looking at advertising for homes that are already under agreement with another buyer.

In most metropolitan areas, there is usually at least one newspaper that is *the newspaper* to use for advertising the sale of real estate. This is the newspaper that contains the most real estate classifieds and is widely utilized by real estate brokers. Most serious buyers, even those using a real estate agent for their home search, will also search this newspaper. However, advertising in *the newspaper* can be expensive, at about $35.00 for only four lines of very small text in a major newspaper printed on three successive days (Friday, Saturday, and Sunday). A small town newspaper will be cheaper.

Because each additional line in the large city newspapers will cost you a few extra dollars, you will find it useful to use abbreviations. However, use abbreviations sparingly as they make the ad copy disjointed and more difficult to read.

If you will be hosting an open house, you should definitely advertise in the large metropolitan newspaper. Serious buyers will scan the section over an early coffee to mark those open houses that they wish to see during the day. This is the newspaper that your home needs to be in.

SELLING TIPS

The weekend, and especially Sunday, is the day that serious home buyers focus their attention on the real estate classified section of the newspaper.

Guide to Commonly Used Abbreviations

Ac	Acre
B, BA or Bath	Bathroom
Balc	Balcony
Br or Bdrm	Bedroom
Cath (cling)	Cathedral Ceiling
CE	Center Entrace
Central air, Cent. A.C, or C.A.	Central Air Conditioning
Col	Colonial
Cont	Contemporary
Crnr	Corner
Cust	Custom
Cent. Vac, or CV	Central Vacuum
DR	Dining Room
Fnc'd	Fenced
Fin LL	Finished lower level (basement)
Fl	Floor
FP	Fireplace
FR	Family Room
Gar	Garage
Ht	Heat (Heating system)
HW	Hardwood (floors)

IG (pool)	In-ground (pool)
In-law	In-law apartment
K or Kit	Kitchen
Loc	Located or Location
LL	Lower Level
LR	Living Room
Mstr or Msr (Br or Bedrm)	Master Bedroom
Mstr or Msr Ste	Master Suite
Nghbrhd	Neighborhood
Ofc	Office
OH	Open House
Pch	Porch
Renov	Renovated
S/E	Split entry
Sit	Situated
Sq ft or sf	Square fee
Spac	Spacious
TH	Town House
Ugrd	Underground (sprinkler)
Updts	Updates
W/	With
W/D	Washer and Dryer
Win	Windows

Local newspapers

The smaller, local newspapers are also a wise choice. Although they are not as widely used by serious buyers, local newspapers allow you to efficiently target a certain area from where you think your buyer is likely to come. As a result of knowing your current neighbors, perhaps you have noticed a trend of where people who move into your town previously have lived. You can use your knowledge of these moving patterns to your advantage. For example, my office is located in the town of North Reading, Massachusetts, a town that is about 15 miles north of Boston. While it is true that some families have moved from one home in town to another home, many families who buy a home in North Reading have come from one of the communities just north of Boston, such as Revere, Medford, Saugus, Malden, Wakefield and Stoneham. These towns would be prime advertising markets for someone selling their home in North Reading.

Place your advertisement in either the local newspaper for a certain targeted town, or if available, in a regional newspaper that covers and circulates among the group of targeted towns. Because the advertising rate is less, you may want to increase the text of your ad and even add a prominent photograph.

If you have noticed a trend of young individuals just out of college and young married and childless couples moving in, you may want to target your market by placing an ad in the local university's newspaper and in various local neighborhood newspapers. Chances are the advertisement in the more local newspapers will not be so bunched together with dozens if not hundreds of other real estate classifieds. This will allow you to reduce the number of abbreviations used and really write an appealing description.

The Internet

The World Wide Web has forever changed many facets of life as we know it. Never before in the history of man have we been able to have so much information so readily available at our fingertips. In only the past decade, the advent of the Internet has drastically changed our ability to compare prices and book airline tickets for travel, obtain information on our favorite hobby, read and investigate current events and news articles, and research information from governmental agencies. The Internet's role in the advertising and marketing of homes by owners is no less phenomenal.

A recent *Google* Internet search using the key words *sell home by owner advertising* yielded 594,000

> **SOLD**
> **FOR SALE**
> # SELLING TIPS
>
> With a potential buyer coming from a town or two away, chances are he or she will be keeping his or her same job. This type of buyer would love to hear about the ease of access to nearby major routes and highways for convenience of commuting purposes.

> **SOLD**
> **FOR SALE**
> # SELLING TIPS
>
> Real Estate Agencies advertise their listings in their local town's newspaper not so much to attract buyers from that town, but rather to demonstrate their presence in town so as to advertise themselves with other homeowners in town. Because of this, homeowners selling their own homes have a distinct advantage in being able to advertise more strategically and efficiently.

results. Needless to say, there is a tremendous amount of resources available online for the *by-owner seller*. Some sites will sell you signs and paraphernalia to use in your marketing. Some will provide general information and suggestions for by-owner sellers. Many of the sites serve as a substitute to the real estate agent's *Multiple Listing Service* (MLS) by acting as the marketplace for homeowners seeking to sell their own home and prospective homebuyers seeking to buy a home.

The marketplace websites differ according to a few major variables, namely:

◆ geographic area;
◆ cost;
◆ marketing assistance; and,
◆ MLS access.

Geographic Area

The difference in sites based on geographic area coverage can be broken into two basic catagories:

◆ national sites and
◆ regional sites.

National by-owner listing sites are those that accept listings for homes in all or many of the states throughout the country. Regional sites cater only to a particular city, state, or region (e.g. New England). When a buyer attempts to locate by-owner homes for sale on the Internet, he or she will find the national sites to be more prominently displayed. The national sites themselves are often of a higher quality, more user-friendly, and of better general appeal.

The regional sites offer home listings for a particular geographical area. These regional sites are often affiliated with a national site. For example, the national site, **www.2buyhomes.net** has several smaller, regional sites such as **www.atlantafsbo.com** and **www.houstonfsbo.com.** Other regional sites are independent from other sites, but are often affiliated with mortgage lenders.

Although they do not have the web prominence and cosmetic appeal of their national-site counterparts, the regional sites are able to advertise heavily on radio, television, and in newspapers on the local scene. Consequently, prospective buyers, when online, will know to go directly to that particular site and forego the web search process.

Since the overwhelming odds are that your buyer will come from the local market and not from a different part of the country, utilizing regional sites is a good bet. Pay attention to the radio or television commercials. If you hear a healthy amount of advertising for a regional site, this is the one in which you should list your home. In effect, by advertising itself, the regional site is subsidizing the marketing expenses for your home.

Cost

Unlike a real estate agency, which will insist on an *exclusive listing agreement* (wherein the owner must pay a commission to the agency when the home sells regardless of whether the agency is the one that finds the buyer or not), you are free to list your home on as many websites as you wish. Your main concern, however, should be cost. Most sites charge a monthly fee for each month your home is advertised on the site. Typically, the monthly fee is in the $30.00 to $80.00 range. This will generally include a generous, but finite word allowance and photos.

The websites also generally offer a flat fee for continuous advertising until your home is sold. With sites that offer this additional choice, the *until it sells* flat rate fee averages about three times the site's one month charge. So, unless you are real confident that your home will sell within three months, its wise to use the *until it sells* option.

Some sites affiliated with or owned by mortgage lenders, subsidize the sites for their own advertising purposes and therefore offer free web listings to sellers. For example, **www.isoldmyhouse.com** (which is owned and subsidized by a local, large lender) offers free listings for home sellers in Massachusetts and other parts of New England. If you are in an area that advertises a reduced cost or free by-owner listing website, be sure to list your home there.

The websites supplement the basic listing service with other add-ons that may or may not work for you. These extra features may be offered as a component in a one of several package plans. Other times, the extras are offered as additional-fee, *a la carte* selections.

Marketing Assistance

Many, if not most, of these websites will offer to sell you a lawn sign as well as directional signs. Make sure that you see a representational photograph of what the sign looks like before you order it. Be sure to compare the sign's features with those necessary components of a good sign as discussed earlier in this chapter. Sometimes, the website signs are too wordy and too crowded so that it is contains more information than people can possibly read as they pass by.

Some websites, especially many of the regional sites, produce their own free *homes for sale* guides/publications that you find around town in vending boxes. Usually for an additional flat-fee, the websites will allow you to be a *featured* home in either or both the guide publication and/or the website. This makes much sense for sellers of high-end properties as the cost of the featured ad/selling price of the home ratio is quite low and can be easily justified.

A few regional websites also offer the seller the advantage of their large buying power. The sites will place a large classified advertisement in one of several local newspapers. They will allow the homeseller to place an ad within this ad at a significant savings over what would be paid if he or she placed the advertisements directly with the newspapers. This feature is attractive especially if the newspapers selected by the website are newspapers that fit into your marketing plan as discussed earlier.

MLS Access

Many web-listing sites are now offering another dimension in advertising the seller's listing online. In an attempt to broaden the client's visibility, many sites offer the homeowner the opportunity to have his or her home listed on the Realtor's® *Multiple Listing Service* (MLS) network. MLS is the very effective national advertising network exclusively used by member real estate agents in which homes listed for sale are pictured and described in detail by the listing agents and made available to all other member agents. Although the home would still be listed and sold by its owner, real estate agents representing buyers as well as buyers browsing through the popular **www.realtor.com** website would now be able to see the listing. This thereby opens up the two single largest advertising venues for the sale of real estate for your home:

◆ the Internet and
◆ the Realtor's MLS.

Although nonreal estate brokers are not allowed to use the Multiple Listing Service, certain websites have arrangements with local brokers in their coverage areas to pay them a fee for their *sponsoring* the listing on MLS. For a flat rate fee currently averaging between $200 and $600, websites such as **www.2buyhomes.net**, **www.forsalebyowner.com**, and **www.salebyownerrealty.com** offer a hybrid choice of a by-owner listing as well as MLS exposure. The homeowner choosing this option will complete a form online and forward the information to the website's participating local real estate agent who has agreed to work with these by-owner sellers for a flat fee. The agent will then list the home on the MLS, Realtor.com, and other Realtor-only venues.

The philosophy of these cooperating brokers basically boils down to—*If you can't beat them, join them.* Getting a small fee for their minimal work in listing your *for sale by owner* property in the MLS is better than not receiving any part of your business. The agents also hope that if you get frustrated trying to sell the home yourself that, as a result of your introduction to a particular agent, he or she will be on top of your list when it comes time to finding an agency to sell your home.

In order to avail yourself of having your home listed in the MLS, you will have to agree at the outset to the compensation you will pay to a broker who procures your eventual buyer. This compensation information will be stated within the MLS listing and the amount of the commission you offer (in addition to the selling price of your home) will be directly correlated to the interest-level of the agents procuring a buyer. An agent who stands to make 3% of a $500,000 sale (a $15,000 commission) will work more aggressively to find a buyer than an agent who stands to make 2% of a $200,000 sale (a $4,000 commission).

Begin the marketing of your home without the flat-rate, broker-MLS option, especially when you have conditions present evidencing a *seller's market*, such as a low level of inventory of homes for sale, a good economy, low interest rates, and/or rising property values. If, instead you utilize a flat-rate broker-MLS service from the outset and sell your home that way, you will always wonder *what if?—What if I sold the home myself through traditional for sale by owner channels? I would have saved thousands of dollars.* You can always change your marketing plan and choose more expensive options as time passes. (An analysis of the options and dynamics of working with and through brokers is discussed more in depth in Chapter 11.)

Miscellaneous Advertising

Up to now, the traditional advertising venues have been discussed: the lawn sign; newspapers; and, the Internet. Your marketing efforts should not stop there. There are other creative options that will effectively get the word out without breaking the bank.

Photo Postcards

Over the last ten years or so, the look and form of Christmas cards that people send to family and friends has changed dramatically. Now, instead of sending generic cards many people send *photo postcards* of their family or children. These photo postcards tell a *thousand words* updating friends and family visually with the picture. Further, sending the postcard by itself saves the time of licking envelopes and almost half the cost of postage. This concept can and should be used for your marketing of the sale of your home.

First, take a flattering photo of your home. A digital camera should be used as it will provide you with the most versatility. (Refer to Chapter 4 for pointers on taking photos of your home.) Next, bring the disk to your local printer, photograph store, or copy shop and ask them to print it postcard size on postcard stock. On the front of the card, on the top of the photograph, have the store print *For Sale By Owner*. Underneath that, choose a two or three word phrase that sums up your home and gets attention such as *Pristine Colonial*, *Hilltop Views*, or *Finished Basement with in-ground pool*. Underneath this, on the third line, write the home's street address. On the back, hold the postcard long-ways and in the left portion, have printed the text that you use in the *Remarks* section of your listing sheet, together with your telephone number. The right section should be left blank so that you can fill in the addressee's address. About 100 of these postcards should cost you about $50.00 to $75.00 and take only 2-3 days for printing.

Once you have the postcards, mail them to all the families in your neighborhood. People often times are hesitant to publicize to their neighbors that they are selling their home. Maybe they consider it a private matter and not for the neighborhood's consumption. However, you cannot expect to have a successful marketing campaign for your home's sale if those in your very neighborhood do not know about it being on the market. These are the people who would be most interested in knowing that your home is for sale. They also are likely to pass the word on to their family and friends who are looking for a new home.

To find out the names and addresses of your neighbors, go to your town hall assessor's office and ask for the street list for the

SELLING TIPS

Don't forget to mail a photo postcard to that neighbor who loves to gossip—he or she will spread the word for you.

streets in your neighborhood. The list will have the names and addresses of each homeowner.

With the remaining unmailed postcards, post them on the public bulletin board of your local supermarket, YMCA, office break room, commuter train station, bank, post office, coffee shop, town hall, or wherever else people gather.

A sample *Photo Postcard* follows on the next page.

FOR SALE BY OWNER

Pristine Colonial
427 Maple Street, Pleasantville

Year-round resort setting awaits you. Level backyard abutting a private pond. Classic center entrance colonial in move-in condition. New great room with cathedral ceiling, 3 walls of glass, and wrap around deck. Corian counter kitchen, spacious rooms, and gleaming hardwood floors.

Broadcast Email

The email system on your office and home computer is another fabulous method for spreading the word about your home being for sale. Email is fast. You can reach more people in five minutes than you could possibly ever be able to talk with on the telephone in an entire day. On top of this, it costs you nothing. Take advantage of all of your work colleagues, personal contacts, and family and friends listed in your computer's address book.

Your email message, itself, should be concise and could say something like:

Hello, I wanted to let you know that my wife and I are selling our home at [address]. We are not using a broker and are trying to advertise ourselves. If you know anyone who is looking to move into the area and desires a beautiful and spacious colonial in move-in condition and with a beautiful, private yard, please pass the word on. We are attaching our listing sheet to provide you with more information. Please email or call us at: [email address] or [telephone number].

If you want, you could also let your email recipients know that you are offering a reward to the person or persons who refer you the eventual buyer of the home. A $500 to $1,000 reward is large enough to get their attention while still being sensible for you, especially when compared to the broker's commission that you will be saving. If you choose to offer a reward with you email, make sure that you specify that it is a total reward and use language such as—

total reward of $1,000 to the person or persons who refer the eventual buyer to us.

This way, in the unlikely scenario that more than one person claims that he or she was responsible for referring your buyer, you will not be responsible for paying $1,000 to each, but rather only will have to pay out $1,000 total.

Owners of Fixer-Uppers

Some homes can and should be marketed to professional investors instead of, or at least in addition to, the general buying public. Your home may very well be such a home, if your home is very small or older and in need of significant repairs and renovation, and especially if it satisfies one or more of these following criteria:

◆ on a sizeable lot of land;

◆ on a lot with a large frontage;

◆ on a flat lot; or,

◆ in or near a newly developed neighborhood surrounded by larger and newer homes.

A *fixer-upper* home may not be very marketable to the general public. However, there often is a multitude of professional investors, real estate speculators, or tradesmen who would be willing to purchase your home from you. They would seek to either completely renovate your home and sell it again to another buyer with the intention of turning a profit (flipping) or they will tear down (raze) the home in order to use the valuable lot to rebuild a newer and probably larger home to sell for profit. Whatever their intention, you still are deserving of the fair market value of your home and nothing less. In both good and not-so-good real estate markets, these *professional* buyers seek and often find and approach a seller even before the home is advertised for sale (sometimes even before the seller has decided to sell it).

Nevertheless, if you own such a home, you have an additional marketing avenue. Approach at least two or more such professional buyers and have them make you an offer. If you do not know the identity of such buyers, consult with your attorney. He or she likely will know such buyers and you can start the bidding war.

chapter six:
Showing Your Home

Once you have completed your listing sheet, have installed your lawn sign, and have placed your advertisements in the newspaper and online, its now time to show your home to prospective interested buyers. Regardless of how many photographs of your home your prospective buyers see online, or how much they read about it in your listing sheet and in the advertisements, nothing substitutes for physically seeing it and inspecting all of its parts. No one will buy your home site unseen. The home showing is the marketing method that allows interested, prospective buyers to come into your home and view it. There are certain *musts* to conduct a successful showing. Following them will help induce hesitant buyers to become serious buyers and serious buyers to become *agreement-signing* buyers.

There are two distinct ways that a prospective buyer will come to view your home: 1) by calling you as a result of seeing your advertisements or by driving by your home and seeing your lawn sign or 2) having visited your home during an open house. The open house can be the event that sells the home.

THE OPEN HOUSE

The open house is a marketing tool in which the homeowner sets aside a period of time, usually 2-3 hours midday on a Sunday, for interested homebuyers to come and view the property. Midday Sunday is the most popular time frame because it is normally the part of the week when people are most available with free time. A buyer who has enough time to fully view the home is more likely to become an interested buyer. Serious buyers will block out most of the day Sunday to drive around to see as many open houses as they can.

By definition, guests arriving to see an open house do so without an appointment and without calling in advance. This takes away some of the awkwardness that the prospective buyer may have in walking through another's home—especially where it is being hosted by the homeowner and not an agent. The prospective buyer takes consolation that the seller will probably be busy with other buyers and therefore will not be the object of the seller's possible hard-sell tactics. Instead, he or she can view the home in a more laid-back setting, probably along side other homebuyers. However, this very characteristic, the potentially numerous parties viewing the home at the same time, is a great dynamic for the seller.

A buyer who views a home at a private showing may have a different reaction if viewing the same home with six other parties at an open house. At the open house, the buyer's competitive juices are likely to flow, driving him or her to be a little more aggressive than he or she otherwise would normally be. The presence of the other people subconsciously may make the buyer think the following.

- ◆ My fondness for the home is confirmed. It is an appealing home, and the seller's asking price is reasonable or else the others would not be here. It is a home worthy of my offer.
- ◆ If I were to buy it and then, sometime down the road, it became time for me to sell it, I could expect a similar crowd of potentially interested buyers.
- ◆ At least one of these other people is going to move ahead and offer on this home. If I do not move now, I stand to lose it. And when I do make an offer, it probably needs to be close to my top offer or one of these other interested persons will outbid me.

The open house can be a very powerful marketing tool. It is quite common to see multiple offers and a bidding war start as a result of one open house. Although this is especially true in a seller's market, an open house can be effective even in a slow economy, as long as there are other people at the open house.

Savvy sellers may want to exploit this dynamic by having a few friends or family members over at the time of the open house and walk around as interested buyers. In addition to help entice interested buyers, your friends and family will serve as additional sets of eyes to protect your personal belongings and discourage extra-snoopy visitors.

A homeowner selling by-owner, should expect the great majority of the people who come to the open house will not be accompanied by a real estate agent. *For Sale By Owner* open houses tend to largely draw buyers not using agents. They either will not be working at all with an agent or, if they are working with an agent, they will have had found your open house themselves as a result of their seeing your advertisement and not called their agent. An agent who is working with buyers will rarely lead them and accompany them to view your home. The reason for this is that an agent generally can comfortably rely on receiving a fee only on those homes that are being sold by another agent on behalf of the home owner. However, do not let this fact dissuade you. A *National Association of Realtors* survey found that less than half of all buyers found the home that they ultimately purchased by using an agent.

ADVERTISING YOUR OPEN HOUSE

There are two principal and fail-safe places for advertising an open house—the Sunday metropolitan newspaper and the lawn sign.

The Right Sunday Newspaper

There typically is one newspaper in your area that is considered *the* place to advertise a home for sale. If you do not know which newspaper this is, either ask someone or buy a few of your local Sunday newspapers and find out which one has the most comprehensive real estate classifieds section. This is the newspaper in which you want to advertise your open house. When advertising an open house, you can start by using the same text for your regular newspaper advertisement, but you will need to also include a few more tidbits of information. Include:

◆ that there is an open house;
◆ the day of the open house;
◆ the time period for the open house; and,
◆ your address.

If the newspaper that your ad appears in is a daily newspaper, then you do not need to worry about the date. Your ad can merely say *Sunday* or *Today*.

As a result of the extra information required for the *open house advertisement*, as opposed to your regular ad, you should expect to pay a little more money.

Make Your Lawn Sign Work

The second way to advertise the open house is with your existing lawn sign. As you may recall from our discussion of the lawn sign, two of the main components of a good sign are the *rider sign* as well as the *directional signs*. These two components prove their worth with the open house.

The rider sign is that smaller sign that acts to provide ancillary information about the home. On the traditional *T-sign*, the rider sign slides right into a groove on top of the horizontal post. At the time you have your sign designed and printed, you should have a rider sign printed stating, *Open House Sunday*. Leave room at the end of the text so that you can stick on removable numerals for the start and end time of the open house to suit your needs when the time arrives. If you have more than one open house, you may want to tweak the start and/or end times based on your prior experience.

The morning of the open house, you will want to set up your directional signs. These are the smaller signs that have a large arrow pointing to the direction of your home. There are two basic types—those that say *Home for Sale* or those that say *Open House*. On the morning of the open house, place as many of the *Open House directional signs* as are needed to guide your visitors from each major route to your actual road. If you put the signs out any earlier, you will chance vandalism. Place the signs on the side of the road where they can be seen from both directions of travel. Do not hide them in tall grass or allow them to be hidden by a tree or road sign.

Finally, on the morning of the open house, tie 3 to 6 brightly-colored balloons to the mailbox, fence, tree, or railing at the front of your home. This, along with your lawn sign, will surely distinguish your home as being the *open house*. In addition, and especially if your home is on a well-traveled road, passersby who were not intending to come to your open house, may have their attention altered by the colorful balloons and it may be just enough to tempt them to drop in.

SETTING THE TIME OF YOUR OPEN HOUSE

When selecting a time period for the open house, take a look at the times for the other advertised open houses in your area. You may want to select the same time period and then add on some additional time before and/or after. For example, if it is customary for open houses in your area to run from 1:00 to 3:00, you may want to make the extra effort and run your open house from 12:30 to 3:30 or noon to 4:00. This additional time may allow those buyers who visited other open houses to come to yours as well, either before or after.

You want to make it easy for buyers to come in. After all, the larger the number of viewers, the greater the chance for a solid offer. Moreover, as a *for sale by owner* seller, you should welcome price-sensitive, comparison shoppers—because you have an incredible built-in advantage of not having to pay a real estate broker's commission.

PREPARE FOR THE SHOWING

When it comes to the open house and the private showing, *for sale by owner sellers* have a sizeable advantage over those sellers using agents. Many times agents appear to show your home to a prospective buyer when you are not home, thereby not allowing you to adequately prepare. Other times, if you are home, the agent will call you to let you know that he or she is preparing to show your home, literally giving you five minutes notice. Owners selling their own homes can make appointments that allow them ample time to prepare the home to their liking. Before each private showing or open house, perform the

SELLING TIPS

Let's say your home and your neighbor's home are both for sale. And, as is common in neighborhoods and sub-developments, let's also assume that your home and your neighbor's home are extremely similar. The homes are very similar in size, age, style, condition, and have very comparable features and amenities. Moreover, the two lots are also similar in size, and shape. If you neighbor is selling his or her home with a broker and has an asking price of $600,000, assuming a broker's 6% commission, you could assign a price as low as $565,000 for your home and still come out of the transaction with more money than your neighbor. If your house is priced $35,000 less than your neighbor's identical house, your home should sell first.

following tasks to increase the likelihood of having a successful showing and to leave the buyer with a favorable impression.

Remove Pets from Your Home

While pets can be cute and loveable, they can be a significant distraction to buyers as they attempt to view your home. When they see pets walking around your home, buyers will be wary about pet dander and odors throughout the home. Again, this all relates back to the premium buyers place on clean and neat homes. Moreover, if you have dogs, they may react to the strangers in your home quite hostily and either bark incessantly, or worse, charge and jump on your guests. Your buyers will be unable to concentrate on your tour and presentation. As a result of the less than hospitable environment, the buyers will rush through their viewing and leave.

Bring your pets to a friend or family member for the duration of your showing. If you bring the dogs to the neighbors, make sure they are kept inside so they will not be tempted to bark when they see your guests arrive. After you have removed the pets, remove all of their paraphernalia, including litter box, food and water bowls, toys, leashes, and beds. To a non-pet lover, these can be unsightly.

Perform a Cursory Outside Inspection

If there are items of litter strewn about, pick them up and throw them in a garbage bag. If there is snow, ice, or leaves in the driveway or walkway to the main entrance, clear it away as it is both an eyesore and a safety hazard to your guests. If you have a garden hose, make sure that it is neatly rolled and stored out of sight. Clear out any children's toys as well.

No Children Allowed

Although no one should mistake my equating small children with animals, in this particular situation, the two need to be treated similarly. Small children and babies are adorable, but their presence during a showing can only be negative. Even if the children are wonderful and quiet, the attention that the buyer gives to them means less attention given to the matter at hand, your home. If they are not so wonderful and quiet during the showing, they can cause the buyer to be distracted, lose interest, and cut their tour short.

Pick Up All Loose and Misplaced Objects

Toys, laundry, footwear, dishes, food, newspapers and magazines, and mail are a potential hazard for those walking around, as well as an eyesore. Also, make all of the beds. Although deep down buyers know that the *mess* does not come with the house, subconsciously they will attribute unfavorable qualities to you as well as your home.

Check All Closets

If they are bulging at the seams, pull out as much of the clothes, shoes, hats, belts, linen, cleaning supplies, board games, and other articles as is necessary to make the closet look neat and orderly. Place the excess items in the trunk of your car or some other out-of-sight location. Bulging closets are a signal to your buyer that the house is too small and lacks storage—an amenity that buyers universally value.

Clean

Dust and/or wipe down all surfaces, including furniture, kitchen, and bathroom counters. Sweep all floors. Wipe all mirrors after applying glass cleaner. With carpeting, sprinkle carpet deodorizer and vacuum to give the room a fresh and clean aroma. Glistening surfaces and mirrors and clean and fresh-smelling carpets are a symbol of your respect for your buyers. Buyers, in turn, will value your home more if you show that you value it.

Keep the Place Warm

If it is cold outside, put the heat on throughout the house to a comfortable 68 to 72 degrees. Also, if you have a fireplace, consider putting it on. If you have a wood-burning fireplace, try using an artificial log instead of wood. It burns at the right pace and will not need your constant attention. The warmth will demonstrate to your buyers that your heating system works well to keep the home cozy in the cold weather. It also helps turns a *house* into a *home* by generating a feeling of comfort and protection—a mood that buyers need to feel before they can be enticed to buy.

Keep the Place Cool

In the warm and hot weather, the home should not be such that you and the buyers will perspire as you tour the home. If you do not have central cooling, consider buying one or more window air conditioning units to keep the home at a comfortable temperature. Otherwise, avoid showing your home during the hottest parts of the day.

Let in Fresh Air

In cool or moderate-temperature days, or on summer mornings, open several windows in the home to allow the fresh air inside. This should especially be done if you have pets, babies, or if someone smokes in the home. On days when it is too cold or too hot to keep the windows open for long, enhance the air inside the home with the scented oil plug-in products that are sold in stores. Use only the same fragrance sparingly throughout the home and not in the kitchen. Do not use too many as it will cause you and your guests to gasp.

Turn on the Stereo

If you have a home sound system with speakers throughout the home, place multiple easy-listening CDs in your player, such as jazz, classical, instrumental, or new age. If you do not have a home-wide sound system, consider turning on various stereos and radios that you have throughout the home to the same easy-listening radio channel. The volume should be understated—not loud enough to interfere with normal conversation. The soothing music that your guests hear from room to room will be a pleasant backdrop to their viewing and will make the home sound and feel like a showplace. Additionally, if you live near a main street, near an airport, near a popular spot on the road where children play, or near a park, the music will aid in blocking this noise out.

Turn off the Television

Unless you have a large state of the art plasma wall screen, which would help demonstrate the functionality of a certain room, avoid putting on the television. The audio coupled with the visual aspects of the television will distract your presentation of your home.

Turn on the Lights

A light and airy home are highly sought after qualities for buyers. A lot of light tends to make people happy and more alive, a good idea when you are look-ing to have a person part with hundreds of thousands of dollars. Open the blinds and shades of all of the windows throughout the home. (If a window on the side of the house overlooks the town dump, it would not be a bad idea to leave this one closed.) Additionally, turn on most of the light fixtures and lamps throughout the home, even if it is during the day.

Add Visual Appeal

Buy some assorted fresh cut flowers and arrange them in vases throughout the home. Also, light some candles and place them in attractive candle holders in selected rooms, including the bathrooms.

Design a Sign-in Sheet

For open houses, place a sign-in sheet on a desk or table close to the front entrance. This way you will have two chances of getting the guests to provide you with their information, when they come in and when they leave. A suggested sign-in sheet appears below.

Date:

Time	Name	Address	Telephone Number	How did you hear about our home?

You also can use this form to record information when people call to make appointments to individually see your home. You will need this information for a few different of reasons.

First, the list will provide you with *contact information* so that you can follow-up with those people who came to see your home. For example, if you detected that certain people were serious and very much liked the home, but perhaps thought the price was too high, you could call those viewers back to inform them of your decision to lower the price.

Secondly, this list will disclose to you from which towns and areas your buyers are coming. This may influence you to boost your advertising in this area if you think that it is ripe with potential prospective buyers.

Thirdly, the list will reveal how the buyer learned of your home being for sale. This may allow you to refine or revise your advertising campaign.

Finally, if you ever decide to sign a contract with an agent to sell your home, the list of people who have been to your home or called to see your home will be very useful. You could attach your lists as an exhibit to the agent's listing agreement. In the contract itself, you then could insert additional language that no commission (or a reduced commission) would be due the agent if one of the named prospects were to eventually buy your home. It is a commonly-accepted practice to list the names of those individuals you procured with *your* marketing efforts and make an exception from the requirement to pay an agent a full commission if one of them were to eventually buy your home.

Develop a Small Portfolio

A small portfolio with information on your home should be prepared to hand to your buyer when he or she enters your home. The portfolio should be an attractive binder that you can purchase at a department or office supplies store. The portfolio should be placed adjacent to the sign-in sheet during open houses and personally handed to your buyer at a private showing. It should consist of the following documents that will answer most of your buyer's questions regarding your home.

The Listing Sheet

The listing sheet will be most helpful to your buyer as he or she tours your home, as it will allow him or her to confirm that what they read on the sheet is accurate and better explain what they see. The listing sheet with your home's prominent photo will allow them to better remember your home in the days following their viewing and will assist them to compare your home to the others that they have viewed. (see Chapter 4 for more on listing sheets.)

The Survey/Plot Plan

Insert in each portfolio, a copy of your home's plot plan or survey. This document is a one-page diagram of the shape and dimensions of your lot and where your home and other structures (pool, shed, garage, etc.) are on it. The plot plan is drafted by a licensed land surveyor or civil engineer. You likely would have obtained a plot plan when you purchased your home. By seeing this document, your buyer will be able to independently confirm your description of the size and shape of the lot.

Highlight Sheet

Insert a highlights page in the portfolio. This can include positive information that you would like buyers to know, but that does not quite fit within the confines of the listing sheet. You should include recent updates, information about the local school system, and other valuable information that a buyer would want to know. The highlight sheet is your opportunity to detail your home's great selling features. These are the items that made you want to buy this home.

Chances are some of your guests are not coming from within the same town or neighborhood, and may know little about your town. Every town has certain qualities that distinguish it from others and of which its residents are proud. These are the type of things to list on the highlight sheet. But be careful. Anything that you put in writing should be accurate. Do your homework first and research through past issues of your town's local newspaper or search the Internet for your towns statistics using the key words, *statistics, towns, [your state]*. State the name of your source on the highlight sheet to give credence to the information and so that you can remember where you obtained it if asked. A sample *Highlight Sheet* follows on the next page.

2485 Park Street, Sunnyville
Highlights

RECENT UPDATES

2004:   New asphalt roof, 2nd layer

2004:   New ceramic tile floor in kitchen

2003:   New carpet in family room installed

2003:   New deck built

2002:   Master bath remodeled

2002:   Main bath remodeled

2001:   New kitchen cabinets installed

2000:   New heating system installed

MAINTENANCE

Home painted in May of 2000

Septic System emptied each November

Fireplace professionally cleaned every other September

Driveway last sealed in June of 2002

A GLANCE AT THE TOWN

Part of the Bonito Elementary School District

School is the newest in town, built in 1998*

Student-teacher ratio last year of 12 to 1*

Sunnyville:

- 12 miles/25 minutes to Metropolis
- Lowest residential tax rate of the five surrounding towns*
- Sunnyville High School:
    - placed in top 10% in state in SAT scores in last 5 years*
    - 84% of seniors continue on to 4 year schools*
    - hockey league champions last two years
- 3 supermarkets, 2 department stores, and 5 banks within 2 mile radius of home
- Home to 2 Italian, 2 Chinese, 1 Thai, 1 Mexican, and 4 seafood/continental restaurants

*Source: The Sunnyville Weekly Journal 2003 year end report

Photos

When the buyer goes back home at the end of a long day of open houses, he or she may have viewed several homes. He or she may have difficulty remembering how your home looked on the inside and on the exterior. Color photographs of your home, therefore, are a great touch for the portfolio.

If you cannot have original prints, make good quality color copies. For the inside, choose three or four rooms that you would like to highlight. Before you take the photographs, make sure that the rooms are very tidy and that there is plenty of natural or artificial light. Ideally, the photos of the exterior will be of different angles of the home (front view, side view, and back yard).

Additionally, if you are selling your home during the winter months, consider inserting previously taken photos of the exterior grounds during the lush spring and summer months. The photos, especially the ones that obviously were taken before you placed your home for sale, will reveal your pride in the home—a quality that buyers value.

Contract

Finally, insert a contract form inside the portfolio. The name and form of this document varies from state to state. It is known as the *Offer, Contract to Purchase, Deposit Receipt, Purchase and Sale Agreement, Purchase Contract, Binder, Sales Contract,* or other similar titles.

If you have decided to let your attorney or someone else handle all negotiations and dealings with the prospective buyer, print up a short memo to attach to the offer instructing them how to contact him or her.

Also in the memo, include instructions on how they can fill out the contract form to your satisfaction. (This will be more fully explored in the Chapter 7). In the majority of cases, buyers will attend an open house or visit the home on a showing without a broker. Therefore, you must assume that they are not very experienced in the process of home buying. Your efforts in foreseeing this and assisting them with having the right

SELLING TIPS

If you are hosting an open house, bake some cookies or an apple pie shortly before the open house is set to start. The wonderful aroma will be a great welcome for your guests as they walk into your home and will make the home feel homey. Plus, this thoughtful midday snack will be appreciated and make you *and* your home stand out.

form together with easy-to-understand instructions will be welcomed by the buyer and will protect you against the buyer feeling too confused and intimidated to make an offer.

CONDUCTING THE TOUR

If you have complied with all or even most of the above suggestions, you have set the groundwork for a successful showing or open house. Now, you can focus on providing your guests with a guided tour of your home.

A good showing definitely increases the likelihood of a sale. However, you do not need to be a masterful salesman. A house is an open and obvious item. A buyer can easily determine its location, style, size, basic lot size, topography, general condition, number and type of rooms, and features all without your having to say a word. Overpowering salesmanship is not needed, and most likely will have a counterproductive effect. A seller who is aggressive or appears to be trying too hard will cause the buyer to think that the seller is, for some reason, not confident of the product and that, therefore, there must be a problem with the home.

Know Your Product

The only *skill* that you need is the same one that makes you the most eminently qualified person to sell your home—your knowledge of the home resulting from your ownership and occupation of it. This is an advantage that you have over everyone else, including even the most successful agents. It is all too common for prospective buyers to ask the agent conducting a showing or an open house a question that the agent cannot answer. At that point, the agent must call the expert—the homeowner. Be confident that your first-hand knowledge of the home is all the skill that you need.

Prior to the showing, go through the home yourself, room by room, and familiarize yourself with what things you want to point out to the buyer at what points. Serious buyers will be eager to learn about the noteworthy features and conveniences in your home that are not so obvious. Conveying this information to the buyer will demonstrate your sophistication, your sincerity, as well as your pride. If you have lived in the home for a short period of time and/or are not familiar with the home's specific features, ask a friend who is a carpenter or tradesman to review the home with you prior to the showing.

Plan a Route

There is a mini-science behind how best to show a home. For starters, be sure to have your guests enter through the main entrance. Illuminate only the lantern in front of the main entrance, place a directional sign to the main entrance, or physically greet your guests outside and take them through the main entrance yourself. First impressions count for a whole lot, and your guests should enter through the door that gives the best presentation. If you have more than one floor, after the first floor, proceed upstairs and not downstairs. You want to show the best parts of the home in order to increasingly build your buyer's interest.

There is a difference of opinion among agents on whether to show the master bedroom, presumably the largest and most elaborate, first or last. However, if you have a truly special master bedroom, you may want to hold it out for last as the dramatic *piéce de résistance*. In addition, introduce bedrooms as the first, second, or third, not by who currently resides in it (for example, Alex's room). Your buyer wants to feel like the home will be for him or her and that it is not *used*.

Set the Right Pace

A common *modus operandi* of *by-owner sellers* is the rapid pace in which they move buyers throughout the home. They overlook the fact that this is the buyer's first time in your home and, unlike you, he or she requires time to *take it all in* and make careful observations. It is up to you as the host/seller to set a methodical pace to the tour. In order to help ensure this, have a pre-planned list of points you want to make at each room on your way through the home. For example, in the 3rd bedroom, you can discuss how the presence and location of the outlets and telephone jack give the buyer the option of using it as an office. In the 2nd bedroom, you can discuss the plaster walls help sound proof the room. In the master bedroom, you can inform the buyer that the custom made curtains will stay and that the ceiling fan operates with a remote. This will educate the buyer, while forcing you to slow down the pace.

Do not leave the room to go to the next room until your buyer gestures that he or she is ready to move on. The longer the buyer stays in the home to view it, the better the chance that he or she will make an offer.

In addition to giving your buyer time to see the home, make sure to also give him or her room. Sellers who sell their own home can often get too *caught up in the moment* when showing their home. While intending to be informative and helpful, they may come across as too overpowering and thereby frighten a buyer.

One common example of this typically occurs when the seller is constantly tripping over the buyer during the entire tour of the home. An astute seller will know when to provide information and when to simple back up and let the buyer look around. This is especially necessary when the buyer is with his or her spouse and/or family. Let them have the space to talk, whisper, or gesture to each other. A stifling seller will annoy the buyer, which may lead to the buyer having a negative impression of the home.

Sell Yourself

In psychology, the *halo effect* is a phrase that is used to describe how people attribute positive qualities, such as intelligence and competence, to physically attractive people. An extension of the halo effect is true with the sale of homes and especially with homes being sold by-owner. If the buyer finds you to be a genuinely warm and friendly person, it is more likely that he or she will transfer this positive reaction to your home.

Use this principle to your advantage. Welcome your buyers into your home and show them your hospitality. Even though they are there to view your home, they still are guests. Engage them in light and friendly conversation. Determine at the outset whether you have something in common with them, such as children or familiarity with the town they live in, and use the opportunity to *connect as people* with something in common. This will relieve some of the natural awkwardness.

After you have finished about half of the tour, step into the kitchen and take a break. Offer your guests a drink along with those cookies or apple pie that you just baked. This would be an ideal time to discuss other selling points that are non-specific to your home—such as the school system, the neighborhood, ease of commuting, or nearby stores and restaurants that you enjoy. While initiating interesting conversation, you also will be subtly conveying other reasons why your home is worthy of their consideration.

The conversation will also allow your buyer to better know you as a person and allow him or her to feel comfortable with you. After all, if a buyer does not feel comfortable with you in conversation, he or she will not feel comfortable to make an offer and negotiate the purchase price with you.

DUTY TO DISCLOSE

As with most homes, there are certain to be conditions in yours that can arguably be described as defective, or in some varying degree of disrepair. These conditions, usually referred to as *defects*, are either *latent*, such as a basement that is prone to flood during heavy rains, yet seemingly dry at the time of the showing, or *open and obvious*, such as cracked bathroom tile or a very dated heating system. As a seller, you will need to plan how you will address these defects and what, if anything you will say to the prospective buyer.

In some states, a seller has no obligation (duty) to disclose defects, even those that are latent. Instead, in most of these states, there is only a *duty to respond* honestly to any inquiries by the buyer about your knowledge of a certain condition. It results in a sort of a *don't ask; don't tell* rule. However, in other states, there is a duty for buyers to disclose the home's *material defects* of which they are aware.

A *material defect* is usually defined as one that, had an ordinary and reasonable buyer known about it prior to the purchase, would have caused him or her to change his or her course of conduct. For example, the basement being prone to flooding during heavy rains would be a material defect if an ordinary and reasonable buyer, having known about this condition prior to making an offer, would not buy the home or possibly would have made only a reduced offer.

There exist some laws that regulate disclosure procedures depending on the specific issue involved. Some states require that sellers disclose all known information regarding the presence of wood-boring insects. Others require a disclosure relating to the amounts of radon (a gas that emanates from out of the earth beneath the home that has been determined to cause cancer and other health problems) detected inside the home. In addition, there is a national requirement that all sellers disclose what they know about any *lead paint* in the home by providing the buyer with a written, signed report. (The lead paint disclosure is covered in more depth in Chapter 7.)

The best advice is to check with your attorney about what is required in your state. A good attorney who is hired prior to your marketing the property, will inform you as to your state's *disclosure laws* and how to comply without being prompted.

FOLLOWING-UP

After each prospective buyer finishes the tour of your home and leaves, you will be able to combine your observational powers and your intuition and make a pretty good calculated guess as to their level of interest. On either the guest log or on a separate piece of paper, assign a value between one and five, with five being the highest, representing how interested each buyer seemed. You should also write down some notables to help you match a name with a face and for possible future *talking points* with this buyer. These are things that you either observed or learned in your meeting with the prospective buyer. Examples include physical appearance, family members present, the topics of your discussion, specific comments about the home, and the reasons he or she gave for wanting to move/buy a home.

If you do not hear from the people who toured your home, call the ones who rated most highly on your list. Or, if the list is small, call everyone. Introduce yourself and tell them that you were happy to have had them show interest in your home. Ask them if they had any further questions about your home. If they do, this is a good sign. It means that they have not ruled out your home as a possible purchase, so answer their questions with patience and care. The prospective buyer may ask questions seeking to determine the interest level of others. Remember, it is very appealing and reassuring for buyers to hear that others are quite interested in your home. So, if true, let them know of other visitors, requests for showings, calls, and offers, if any. Tell them that you would be happy to have them tour the home again if that would help them in their decision-making. Refer to some of your saved *talking points* for this buyer. Remember, by selling yourself as a warm, engaging, and courteous person, you will be doing much to sell your home.

If they do not want to see the home again but are outwardly interested, ask them if they are considering making an offer. You may also want to offer that you will meet with them to fill-out or retrieve the offer (with the deposit), or welcome them to call your attorney to fill out the offer.

If you do meet with the buyer to retrieve the offer, have a ready reason, if necessary, as to why you cannot accept it right then and there. Tell the buyer—*I need to discuss this with my wife,* or *I have another showing later today and will get back to you after that.* This will relieve any of the pressure that the buyer may place upon you to accept the offer on the spot.

chapter seven:
Arranging the Deal

With a home that is priced right and marketed well, it is only a matter of time before a ready, willing, and able buyer steps forward and makes an offer. You are now entering the critical negotiation and contract phase. This is a very precarious phase for a couple of important reasons. First, you will face the daunting task of reeling in the buyer to *close the deal,* while also trying to protect your legal and financial interests. Secondly, there are dozens of potential pitfalls in the process and in the contract language and terms. Your failure to anticipate and guard against these pitfalls will increase the likelihood of a potentially significant setback. For these reasons, it is always recommended that the seller obtain the services of a competent real estate attorney. (One should be obtained prior to your signing any document.)

This chapter, like the book as a whole, is not meant to substitute for the advice given by your attorney. The process of entering into a contract for the sale of a home in our country varies considerably from state to state. The one rule that is valid throughout the land is that there is no single, universal process for the sale of a home. Therefore, neither this book nor any other similar book can provide you with all of the nuances that may be applicable in your area. Your attorney will be able to access the facts, issues, and laws in your particular situation and make decisions and give recommendations accordingly. Instead, this chapter aims to provide you with *the big picture* so that you can anticipate the issues that may arise and so that you can be better educated to work with your attorney to protect your interests and ensure a smooth transaction.

PURCHASE AND SALE AGREEMENT

In many parts of the country, it is customary for the terms governing the purchase and sale of a home to be set forth in only one document. This document goes by many names, depending on your area, including *Purchase Agreement, Purchase Contract, Purchase and Sale Agreement.* This book will use *Purchase and Sale Agreement* to describe these documents.

In other areas of the country, it is typical for the parties (the buyer and seller) to use two documents, the second of which is the *Purchase and Sale Agreement.* The first document used in these areas is also called by many names, including the *Offer, Contract to Purchase, Deposit Receipt*, and *Binder.* Keep in mind that these are only the norms, and nothing mandates that you follow suit. For example, it is perfectly fine for you to skip over the *Offer to Purchase* form and go directly to the *Purchase and Sale Agreement* for your sale if you are in an area that normally uses both documents. Similarly, if you live in an area that uses only the *Purchase and Sale Agreement*, it is also perfectly acceptable for you to use an *Offer to Purchase* first. It is the content, and not the style, of the documents that you sign that matters.

Obtaining Contract Forms

One common fear of homeowners considering selling their home by themselves is not having the *preprinted* documents that real estate agents often provide. The preprinted forms provide the seller with a sense of security. Many sellers believe that the preprinted form is the *standard* form, and will protect them from leaving out necessary contract language. Unfortunately, as will be discussed later, there is no *one size fits all* for real estate contracts. Even the real estate agent's forms almost always need to be altered in order to fit your specific situation. However, finding a form to meet your state and local laws as well as your specific situation is an important starting point for *by-owner sellers.*

From Your Attorney

The best place to obtain a contract that is suited for you is to have your attorney draft it. There are plenty of forms in circulation posing as real estate contracts, found either in office supply stores or on the Internet. The problem here is generally two-fold:

◆ the laws and procedures of your particular state or town are not taken into consideration and/or

♦ the facts and issues specific to your transaction are not taken into consideration.

While it is often prudent to market and sell your home without a broker, to also do so without an attorney is unnecessarily risky. An attorney's fee for your sale will cost you only a fraction of what you save by not using a broker. For the sale of a $400,000 home, the $500 to $1,500 attorney's fee is a drop in the bucket compared to the broker's $24,000 fee. Now is not the time to be penny wise and pound foolish. (See Chapter 3 for more information on using an attorney.)

Using an attorney is always recommended, but using an attorney is crucial if one or more of the following factors is true in your situation.

♦ You are buying another home immediately after selling your home.

♦ The buyer is using a buyer's agent.

♦ The buyer is represented by an attorney.

♦ You are selling the home owned by someone who recently died.

♦ You are aware of IRS liens, real estate tax liens, utility liens, court attachments, court judgments, mechanic's liens, or other title problems for your home.

♦ You recently have filed or gone through the bankruptcy process.

♦ You have tenants in your home (whether it is a single or multifamily) and your buyer wants at least one of the occupied units to be sold vacant.

♦ You have are selling a multifamily home.

♦ Your buyer offers to buy your home contingent on selling his or her own home.

♦ Your buyer wants to move into your home before he or she buys it.

♦ You need to continue to live in your home after you sell it.

From Other Sources

If, for whatever reason, you do not choose to have your attorney draft the contracts, there are other sources that, although not as optimal, should suffice. The basic form *Purchase and Sale Agreement* can be used as a starting point. This form, however, may be different in style and context than what is required for your state.

For forms that attempt to comply with your state's laws and norms, search regional listing websites. Many of these regional sites, in addition to having listings for your state and area, may also have acceptable contracts specific for your area.

In addition to these sites, there are also other websites that specialize in legal forms. Some even break down the forms by state. You may want to check out the following sites:

www.uslegalforms.com

and

www.findlegalforms.com.

(Expect to pay a fee in order to download these forms.)

Standard Terms of the Contract

While *Purchase and Sale Agreements* vary in style and content, when you pare them down, they are quite similar. The following are an itemization of the integral parts of the agreement—the *standard terms*. A brief explanation as well as some pointers on how best to make the language work for you is also discussed.

Date

The *date* identifies when the *Purchase and Sale Agreement* is effective. It is ideal to have both parties sign on the same day. If this is not possible, the date should reflect the day when the second of the two parties (usually the seller) signs.

Premises Description

The *description* should include a street address description, a square footage description of the lot (if applicable), as well as a legal description (book and page number of the current deed as recorded at the registry of deeds) of the property being sold. When restating the square footage, you want to be sure to use the word *approximately* as a caveat so that you avoid liability if it later determined by your buyer to be somewhat less.

Parties

The *parties* clause specifies who is doing the selling and who is doing the buying. In addition to the complete legal names of each party, the party's current legal address should be included here. As the seller, be sure that the buyer has reached legal age (in most states this is 18 years) or else the contract may not be binding.

Purchase Price

This section will set forth the total price that the buyer is obligated to pay for the home. However, it also will break down the total to show the amount of the buyer's deposit(s) and when it or they are to be paid. For example, in many states it is customary for buyers to pay a total of 5% of the total price as a deposit. This 5% deposit is paid by the buyer when the *Purchase and Sale Agreement* is signed or when the home inspection contingency has expired. In areas that use an *Offer* as well as *Purchase and Sale Agreement*, the 5% deposit is staggered—with usually a $1,000 deposit given by the buyer with the offer and the balance paid upon signing the *Purchase and Sale Agreement.*

The seller should insist on the buyer paying as high of a deposit as is customary in the area. If the buyer *defaults* (fails to go through with the deal) after signing the *Purchase and Sale Agreement*, retaining the buyer's deposit often will be the seller's only remedy. Therefore, it should be a red flag for the seller whenever the buyer attempts to put down less than what is normal.

The purchase price section will also state with what type of funds the buyer is obligated to pay over to the seller at the time of sale (cash, bank check, certified check, attorney's check, or personal check). This may not even register as a minor concern to the seller at the early stage of the *Purchase and Sale Agreement*. However, it could become a major headache later.

At the *Purchase and Sale Agreement* stage, your buyer may request to be allowed to pay you with his or her bank attorney's or escrow agent's escrow check. This sounds fancy but despite its sophisticated label, they are not good

SELLING TIPS

Suppose that you are selling your home and buying another home on the same day (referred to as *back to back* closings). If you expect to use the proceeds from the sale of your home to buy your new home, the funds from your sale need to be in the form of cash, a certified check, or a bank check. If not, the bank attorney, title agent, or seller will not have *good funds* from you—funds that are not contingent upon clearing. The proceeds from your sale will then not be available for your purchase until they clear, possibly days after you wanted to close on your purchase.

funds like a bank check. So, if you are buying another home within a day or two of selling yours, you should not allow the buyer to pay you in anything other than good funds, especially if you will be buying in a different state than where you are selling. You may even want to include a provision in the *Purchase and Sale Agreement* (or *Offer*) that your buyer's bank attorney or escrow company wire your sale proceeds to you, your bank attorney, or escrow company.

If you do not negotiate the good funds requirement into the *Purchase and Sale Agreement*, you can always check with your lender's attorney or title agent for your new home purchase. Often times, he or she will be able to accept your buyer's lender's attorney's or title agent's check without too much difficulty.

Deposit Held In Escrow

The *Purchase and Sale Agreement* needs to recite that the buyer's deposit will be held in *escrow*. Escrow refers to the process in which the buyer's deposit is placed in the hands of a third person and held by that person until the closing is complete. A buyer who contemplates buying a home offered by a *by-owner seller* already may feel insecure about the process. Having to give 5% of the purchase price directly to the seller a month or more before he or she owns the home is even more disconcerting. Instead, provide in your pre-printed *Purchase and Sale Agreement* for your attorney to hold the deposit.

Attorneys are licensed and regulated by the state and have to abide by a very strict

---

SELLING TIPS

If, in your area, you will use the Offer as well as the Purchase and Sale Agreement, you will note that many of the provisions are first presented and included in the terms of the Offer. These include the price, type of funds, deposit amount, date of closing, and specifics relating to the financing and inspection contingencies. If you accept the Offer with these terms, it will not be possible to modify them unless both parties agree.

Not too many buyers would be willing to change a less restrictive financing contingency and make it more restrictive simply because you so requested. Therefore, if you plan to accept a buyer's Offer, make a quick appointment with the attorney with whom you have already consulted, to review its terms before you sign.

code of professional conduct. Furthermore, attorneys, and especially real estate attorneys, are very well versed in handling escrow funds and in the related protocol. In addition, you should have language in the deposit provision stating that if there is a dispute relating to the deposit, the escrow agent will be required to retain the deposit pending the receipt of mutual instructions by the buyer and seller or a court order. In other words, if you believe that the buyer has breached the contract and is entitled to retain the deposit as your remedy, all the buyer has to do is direct the attorney to hold the deposit and not release it pending the resolution of the dispute. This will help provide the buyer with the needed assurance to move forward in the purchase of your home.

Time for Performance

This section of the *Purchase and Sale Agreement* states the date, time, and place for the closing. The closing is the climax of the purchase and sale process, and, when pared down to its simplest component, is where the seller transfers title to the home, via the deed, to the buyer in exchange for the agreed-upon purchase price.

When agreeing on a date for the closing, do your best to stay away from the last week and especially the last day of the month. The end of the month is notorious for being the busiest (and therefore the most stressful) time to have your closing. Unfortunately, many real estate agents, when writing up offers and *Purchase and Sale Agreements*, have a natural inclination for using the last business day or week as the agreed-upon closing date. Many brokers have only one or two transactions per month so they likely will not have a scheduling conflict. However, many of the other *players* including the buyer's bank, the bank's attorney (or title company), the buyer's attorney, the seller's attorney, the appraiser, the title examiner, the registry personnel, and the moving company tend to have an overwhelming number of closings condensed into a few days at the month's end.

Many agents believe that it helps the buyer with his or her mortgage loan. This really is a fallacy. If a buyer closes on a home on August 31, it is true that he or she will likely only have to pay one day's interest for the last day of August. Consequently, the first payment will be the first day of the second month following—October 1st.

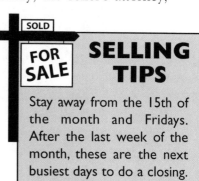

SOLD

FOR SALE

SELLING TIPS

Stay away from the 15th of the month and Fridays. After the last week of the month, these are the next busiest days to do a closing.

However, if the closing is moved back two days to September 2nd, the buyer will have to pay 29 days of prepaid interest at closing, but then will not have to make his or her first mortgage payment until November 1st—an entire extra month. (Some banks, when faced with this scenario, instead will credit the buyer two days worth of interest and have the buyer make his or her first payment on October 1st—further evidencing the non-existence of any advantage for closing at the end of the month.)

No matter how you look at it, closing at the end of the month offers no advantage to the seller. When you consider the strain placed at the end of the month on all of the people whom you will need to give attention to your transaction to help it go smoothly, it makes sense to choose another date.

In choosing a date, you also want to feel certain that the one selected by the buyer works for you. For example, if your buyer wants to *close* on your home on December 9th but you already signed a contract to buy your new home on December 6th, you will have a problem if you need the proceeds from your sale to purchase your new home. If you mistakenly end up in such a predicament, you will have to try to have either your buyer or the seller of your new home voluntarily agree to change the date so that your sale occurs first. Although you are already bound by both contracts, the reality of it is that you cannot buy until you sell. A little financial incentive may be required if the other party is stubborn.

The time of day poses a similar concern. Although the time mentioned is often changed due to the various schedules of the parties involved in the closing, if you are undertaking a back-to-back closing, it is a good idea to insert language to the effect of—

> *Buyer acknowledges that Seller is purchasing another home on the same day and therefore agrees to use his or her best efforts to request that his or her lender and lender's attorney schedule this closing during the morning hours.*

In this time and date section in virtually all *Purchase and Sale Agreements*, the following sentence, or a close derivation thereof, will appear—

> *Time is of the essence.*

This is powerful language for sellers. Without this language, the parties will not be held to the stated date. With this language, the date has a legal bite.

Example: Assume your buyer agreed to purchase your home on May 9th, but as the closing date approached, decided to postpone it because he or she thought that by waiting two weeks he or she could obtain a better interest rate on a mortgage loan. If you do not have this *time is of the essence* language, he or she probably will be able to hold you up. If, instead, you do have this language, you will be able to require the buyer to meet his or her obligations on May 9th, and, if he or she refuses, you will be entitled to the remedy allowed for in the *Purchase and Sale Agreement* for a default by the buyer.

Most typically, the remedy in these types of situations would call for you to retain the buyer's deposit.

Property Included

This part should specifically itemize what structures, improvements, fixtures, and personal property will be part of the sale to the buyer. It is quite standard that any improvements or fixtures that are physically attached to the structure will remain with the property and be sold with the home. Examples include window blinds and shades, shutters, furnaces and heating equipment, plumbing and bathroom fixtures, lighting fixtures, television antennae, trees and shrubs, and if built in, dishwashers and air conditioning equipment.

Structures such as fences, pools, and sheds, unless otherwise stated, remain with the home. Outside of these givens, everything that could be questionable needs to be specifically stated, especially if you seek to take it with you.

You can execute an agreement stating you want to dig up a special shrub or sentimental rose bush to take with you. If you want to take the ornate chandelier, it is typical for the seller to replace it for the buyer with a more basic fixture.

Frequent items of contest include window drapes, the refrigerator, stove, washer machine and dryer, bookcases and shelving, landscaping improvements

SELLING TIPS

If you are feeling a little guilty about being possessive and wanting to keep some of the items, do not feel bad. In some parts of Europe, when a seller sells the home, it is common practice to take just about everything except for the structure itself. This includes all light fixtures, the stove and all appliances, and even the kitchen cabinets.

such as lighting and benches, swimming pool equipment, fireplace accessories, light and outlet plates, and mailboxes. If you want to retain any of these, you will need to state this prior to signing the document.

Deed and Title

This is a very important element of the *Purchase and Sale Agreement*. In this section, the parties agree as to the *type of deed* that will be transferred by the seller to the buyer, as well as the *quality of the title* that the seller must transfer.

Type of Deed

A deed is a written document that evidences ownership of certain real estate. It is a written document that, when a seller sells his or her home transfers ownership (title) to another (the buyer). There are two main types of deeds, a *warranty deed* and a *quitclaim deed*. A warranty deed is one in which the seller guarantees that his or her ownership is free from defects. (In legal speak, the seller *warrants that his or her title is good and clear*.) A quitclaim deed (often mistakenly referred to as a *quick claim* deed) is a deed that passes on title to the buyer but does not guarantee that the title is clear. In some states, a seller using a quitclaim deed warrants that there has been no defect under his or her ownership, but he or she does not make such a representation as to others before him.

The use of each type of deed is largely dictated by the state (or county) where the home is situated and is not typically subject to negotiation by the parties. As the deed is a legal document that needs to be prepared in accordance with laws and local practices and standards, it is typically prepared by an attorney. In fact, in some states, a deed *must* be prepared by an attorney.

Quality of Title

Title, for purposes of the *Purchase and Sale Agreement*, refers to the quality of ownership that the seller is required to pass to the buyer. It is standard for *Purchase and Sale Agreements* to call for the highest quality, by using the words *clear record and marketable title*. For example, assume just prior to selling your home to the buyer, a search at the applicable registry of deeds reveals that you have an outstanding loan and mortgage to the bank. Let's also assume that this is the only defect that was found as a result of the search. You, therefore, would not be in compliance with the clear record and marketable title requirement unless you paid off and *discharged* the outstanding mortgage at the registry of deeds in conjunction with the sale.

Besides outstanding mortgages, other examples of title defects that the seller would need to fix in order to convey clear record and marketable title are:

◆ tax liens;

◆ court attachments and judgments;

◆ mechanic's liens;

◆ tenant's leases; and,

◆ divorce and probate matters.

Conversely, the following are either examples of defects (or encumbrances) in the title that buyers generally will allow to exist when they purchase the home or do not constitute title defects:

◆ zoning or building code violations (although these may be addressed by the buyer elsewhere in the *Purchase and Sale Agreement*);

◆ taxes for the current fiscal year which are not yet due;

◆ with condominiums, all restrictions, easements, and encumbrances referred to in the condominium trust, bylaws, and master deed;

◆ any liens for municipal betterments (installation of sewer pipes) that may be assessed after the date of the *Purchase and Sale Agreement*; and,

◆ easements and restrictions of record that do not substantially affect the current use of the home and land.

Possession and Conditions of Premises

This section allows buyers to recite how the home must appear just prior to the buyer's purchase. If you have a tenant or tenants in the property, this section clarifies whether or not the buyer wants them to remain in possession of the property. The section often also specifies that the home, at the time of the closing, should appear in substantially the same condition as when the buyer signed the *Purchase and Sale Agreement*. The buyer is given the right to have an inspection of the home just prior to closing to determine the seller's compliance. In most states, the risk of loss during the *executory period* is on the seller. In other words, if something happens to the home after the buyer signs the *Purchase and Sale Agreement* but before the closing, the seller has the responsibility of restoring it to its prior condition. To protect against this, the seller should keep a homeowners insurance policy in full effect and not cancel it until the closing has occurred and the deed to the buyer has been recorded.

Additionally, many buyers or buyers' attorneys will include language requiring the home to be in—

> *broom-clean condition free of all personal property, both inside and outside the home, that is not included in the terms of the agreement.*

Because a buyer likely will not recede from these requests, you must be prepared to remove all the contents of your home—including all of those items cluttering the attic, garage, basement, shed, and back yard. *Purchase and Sale Agreements* allow buyers to conduct a last minute *walk-through inspection* of the home just prior to the closing to ensure your compliance with this language.

Remedies in the Event of Default

This section will spell out what one party is entitled to as a remedy if the other fails to uphold his or her obligations.

Seller's Obligation

The major obligation of the seller is to transfer record and marketable title, via the deed to the buyer, on the agreed-upon date. Inevitably, a seller will encounter *title problems* that may hamper or even jeopardize his or her ability to do this. These title problems are revealed after an examination of your title at the registry of deeds and may include:

◆ prior mortgages that still appear *outstanding;*
◆ a lien filed by a contractor who has done work on your home;
◆ a court judgment as a result of a lawsuit that you lost;
◆ a bankruptcy petition that you filed;
◆ a right or claim by some other third party in your title; or,
◆ if the home is being sold soon after the death of a loved one, probate requirements.

The seller is often protected from being in default as a result of an *escape clause* in the *Purchase and Sale Agreement.* If you are unable to convey record and marketable title as a result of one or more title problems within some specified amount of days, then you will be able to apprise the buyer of this and will be able to void the *Purchase and Sale Agreement*. You would return all of the buyer's deposit and the two parties would walk away from the deal without any further obligations to each other.

The escape clause is normally written to require the seller to use *reasonable efforts* to correct the title problem. As you may infer, if you inform the buyer that you are not able to sell the home due to the title defect, the buyer may contend that you did not use *reasonable efforts*. Accordingly, it is recommended that you define this for your protection. Consider using the following language—

> *Reasonable efforts as defined in this provision shall not require the Seller to expend more than $2,000 to cure the title defect, exclusive of voluntary liens.*

Therefore, if a contractor's lien (often referred to as a *mechanic's lien*) in the amount of $10,000 is discovered as part of the title search, even though it is possible to remedy the defect within the 30 days, you have the option of canceling the sale as you would be required to spend more than $2,000 to fix the title problem. As stated in the suggested language, this protection would not apply to *voluntary liens*, which are those liens that you voluntarily and knowingly grant to someone, such as a mortgage to a bank.

If there are no title problems or if the seller remedies any title problem within the allowed time, he or she will have the obligation to sell the home to the buyer. If the seller then fails to transfer title to the buyer, he or she will be in default of the *Purchase and Sale Agreement*. As you may envision, this often happens during periods of rapidly increasing home values, when sellers are tempted to break the deal with their buyer in order to sell to another buyer who has presented a higher-priced offer. The buyer's remedy, if this occurs, is to file a complaint in the appropriate court seeking *specific performance*. Essentially, the buyer would ask the court to mandate that the seller transfer title of the home to him or her.

Buyer's Obligation

The buyer's main contractual obligation is to buy the seller's home. If the buyer fails to fulfill this and there are no further contingencies on which the buyer may rely to void the agreement, the seller may have two powerful remedies. They are:

◆ to keep the deposit paid by the buyer and/or
◆ to additionally seek specific performance requiring the buyer to buy the home as agreed.

Because of drastic effect of the second remedy, it is commonplace for buyers to limit their exposure by including the following language in the contract—

> *If the Buyer shall fail to fulfill the Buyer's agreements herein, all deposits made hereunder by the Buyer shall be retained by the Seller as liquidated damages. This shall be the Seller's sole and exclusive remedy in law and in equity.*

SELLING TIPS

In areas that utilize an Offer as well as a *Purchase and Sale Agreement*, most courts will rule that even if the parties did not come to terms on the more involved *Purchase and Sale Agreement*, the buyer can seek specific performance if the seller accepted the buyer's offer and the offer contained the basic terms, such as the price of the home and the closing date.

With this language included, the seller will only be allowed to keep the deposit and not force the buyer to purchase the home. This additional language requested by the buyer or the buyer's attorney is widely accepted by sellers, and virtually is now standard language. This is because no buyer would want to sign an agreement if he or she stood to both lose a significant amount of money *and* still be required to buy the home.

Moreover, if a buyer is not financially able to buy the home (whether or not this was the cause of the breach of the agreement), it would be an exercise in futility to try to force the buyer to buy it. This is why it is important for sellers to carefully review the buyer's finance contingency requests and follow-up by including the aforementioned suggested protective language.

Buyer's Contingencies

The *Buyer's Contingencies* refer to the two main provisions that allow the buyer to get of the agreementæthe *inspection contingency* and the *financing contingency*. These contingencies usually appear in two separate and distinct sections in the agreement. In addition, if you are in an area that uses the preliminary offer form, in addition to the *Purchase and Sale Agreement*, these contingency provisions may appear in each of the two documents.

Inspection

Most buyers will want to conduct at least some level of inspection on your home before they buy it. The various types of inspection include:

- ◆ termite/pest;
- ◆ radon;
- ◆ lead paint;
- ◆ septic system;
- ◆ water;
- ◆ soil; and,
- ◆ structural.

The language inserted by the buyer will allow him or her to void the contract and obtain all of the deposit back if the results of the inspection do not comply with the standard stated in the contract. In most cases, you should allow the buyer to conduct any of the aforementioned inspections, as to do otherwise would immediately raise a red flag and could cause the buyer to walk away.

Besides the type of inspection requested by the buyer, the other variables that need to be negotiated for the inspection contingency are:

- ◆ the date by which the buyer has to conduct said inspections;
- ◆ the standard by which the buyer may lawfully void the contract; and,
- ◆ the date by which the buyer has to notify you of his or her voiding the contract.

To best suit your needs, strictly limit the buyer to a short period of time by which to both conduct the inspections and to inform you if he or she is backing out of the deal. Ten days is generally sufficient for this. The longer the buyer has to conduct these inspections, the longer he or she is tying you and your home up and preventing you from entertaining other prospective buyers.

There are two distinct standards commonly used to determine if a buyer has the right to void the contract as a result of the inspectionsæthe subjective standard and the objective standard. The *subjective standard* favors the buyer. It states—

> *If the buyer is not satisfied with the results of said inspec-*
> *tion(s), then buyer may give written notification to the seller*
> *prior to the inspection notification deadline and this*
> *Agreement shall be null and void and all deposits shall be*
> *returned to the buyer.*

With this language, the buyer has an absolute escape from the contract. For a buyer who gets a sudden case of the cold feet, this language is the perfect medicine. The buyer can nondescriptly cite to *what the inspector found* and lawfully walk away from the deal with his or her full deposit back.

Therefore, use the *objective standard* language for any pre-printed offers or *Purchase and Sale Agreements* that you give your buyer to sign. This standard may be worded as follows—

> *If the premises contains serious structural, mechanical, or*
> *other major defects, then, at the option of the Buyer, Buyer*
> *may give written notification to the Seller together with a copy*
> *of the written report of the person conducting said inspection,*
> *said person to be a person normally engaged in the business*
> *of conducting home inspections, prior to the inspection noti-*
> *fication deadline, and this Agreement shall be null and void*
> *and all deposits shall be returned to the Buyer.*

The objective standard makes it much more difficult for a nonserious buyer to walk away and keep his or her deposit.

Financing

The second contingency that a buyer customarily will request is for *financing*. Essentially, the buyer is requesting to be excused from having to fulfill his or her obligation of buying your home if unable to obtain a mortgage loan.

There are several different types of mortgage lenders, including conventional, Federal Housing Administrations (FHA), Veterans Administration (VA), and private lenders. As the seller, you want the buyer to have to explore at least the first three on the list before he or she is able to back out of the deal for not qualifing.

The buyer should not waste your time if he or she is not serious about buying your home. The typical standards used in *Purchase and Sale Agreements* (in increasing order of effort needed) are:

◆ reasonable efforts (or diligence);

◆ all due diligence; and,

◆ best efforts (or diligence).

Therefore, make sure the *Purchase and Sale Agreement* requires the buyer to commit to either of the last two standards when applying for a loan. If you use the *reasonable efforts* standard and he or she is not able to obtain a mortgage loan commitment, you will have great difficulty showing a breach in obligations. Despite the wasted days, most likely you will have to return his or her deposit and find another buyer.

Keep your buyer from holding up your sale. Restrict him or her to 30 days or less to attempt to obtain a mortgage loan commitment. In times of a sellers' market, you may want to reduce this to 20 days.

The buyer will have to state within the finance contingency provision the mortgage amount he or she is requesting. Although it varies according to your particular state, a mortgage amount of no more than 80% to 90% of the sales price is customary. The buyer is telling you, that at least 10% to 20% of the money being put down is his or her own money.

A contingency for a mortgage representing 90% or more of the agreed-upon purchase price should be a cause of some concern. This could mean one of two things: 1) the buyer is hoping to qualify for a loan amount outside of normal limits many lenders set and may have difficulty qualifying. The buyer, consequently, has a higher chance of getting denied for a loan, and you have a greater chance of having your sale held up; or 2) the buyer has requested that the contingency be for a percentage or an amount that is artificially higher than what they really need.

Example: Let's say you and the buyer agreed upon a sales price of $350,000. The buyer has $150,000 to put down (not including an additional sum that he or she has set aside for closing costs) and therefore needs a mortgage of $200,000. However, instead of inserting the $200,000 loan amount in the blank space in the finance contingency provision, he or she writes in $250,000. The buyer is doing this to give him or herself an extra cushion of protection. If it turns out that he or she will need a larger loan than the

$200,000 (e.g., if he or she is not clearing as much from the sale of his home as he or she originally thought), then he or she will be covered and will be able to void the deal and get his or her deposit back if the bank will not agree to give him or her the $250,000.

It may be that this offer is the first and only one that you have received in 6 months. In this case, you probably will have to be more acceptable of such protections requested by the buyer. However, if you are in a good market and/or receive multiple offers, you may decide that it is wiser for you to accept someone who, despite having made a lower offer, has either no finance contingency or has one requesting a smaller mortgage loan amount.

The seller, in order to clarify the terms of the financing contingency and to better protect against nonserious or credit-unworthy buyers, can include one or more of the following additional provisions.

- *This Agreement is not contingent upon the Buyer selling any real property. In addition, a mortgage commitment containing conditions shall be deemed a full commitment and shall not relieve the Buyer of his or her obligations under this Agreement.*

- *This Agreement is contingent upon the Buyer, within 10 days of this Agreement, forwarding to Seller a letter from a licensed institutional mortgage lender stating that Buyer is pre-approved for a mortgage loan of the amount and terms requested in the financing contingency section. If the Buyer fails or neglects to forward said letter within the said 10 days, this Agreement shall be rendered void, the Seller and Buyer shall be released of their obligations and the Seller shall return the Buyers deposit.*

- *In order to avail him/herself of the protections under the financing contingency provision, the Buyer, on or before the deadline date specified in said section, agrees to provide the Seller with written confirmation from the lender of his or her inability to qualify for the requested loan.*

Seller's Contingencies

Depending on the specific situation, you may want to or need to include language in the *Purchase and Sale Agreement* (and, if used, the *Offer*) making your obligation to sell the home to the buyer contingent on one or more occurrences.

As discussed earlier in the book, you may want to be able to cancel the deal if you are not able to find a new home for yourself. In this case, you can try to negotiate a *seller's finding new home* contingency. Do not expect most buyers to agree to this, especially those who are working with an attorney or an agent, or when you are in a buyer's market. Commonly-used language for this contingency is—

> *The seller's obligations pursuant to this Purchase and Sale Agreement are contingent upon the seller finding suitable housing and executing a Purchase and Sale Agreement (or closing) on such suitable housing on or before [date].*

There are also a couple of circumstances wherein you may need to insert a contingency. If you are selling the home of a loved one who recently died and the home is part of his or her estate, you may need to obtain a court order (sometimes referred to as a *license to sell*) in order to lawfully sell the home. Also, if you are selling a condominium, the condominium association may have a *right of first refusal*. This means that although you have found a buyer, the condominium association may be able to step in and purchase your unit instead (usually for the exact price that your buyer offered you.) If either of the above applies to your situation, you will need to write contingency language into the *Purchase and Sale Agreement* so that you may be lawfully excused from selling the home to the buyer if you do not obtain the court's permission or the condominium association wants to exercise its right of first refusal.

A sample Purchase and Sale Agreement follows on the next page.

Purchase and Sale Agreement

1. Date of this Agreement:

2. Premises:
City or Town: Land Area:
Street Address:
Legal Description:
Seller's Title Reference: Book: Page:
Assessor's Map Reference:

3. Seller:
Address(include street and mailing address, if different):
Phone: Social Security Number(s):
Record Owner (if different)
Seller's Attorney: Phone:
Address:

4. Buyer:
Address:
Phone   Social Security Number(s):
Buyer's Attorney: Phone:
Address:

5. Purchase Price: $ _____
   Paid as Follows:
      Deposit Paid to Date: $ _____
      Deposit Paid Upon Signing of this Agreement: $ _____
      Additional Deposit, if any, to be paid on: $ _____
      Balance of Purchase Price due on Closing Date: $ _____

6. Escrow Agent:
Address:
Deposits to be held in: _____ non-interest bearing account
                               _____ interest-bearing account

7. Closing:
Date:
Place:

8. Buildings, Structures, Improvements, Fixtures
Included in the sale as a part of said premises are the buildings, structures, and improvements now thereon, and the fixtures belonging to the SELLER and used in connection therewith including, if any, wall to wall carpeting where installed, all venetian blinds, window shades, curtain rods, screens, screen doors, storm windows and doors, awnings, shutters, furnaces, heating equipment, stoves, ranges, oil and gas burners and fixtures appurtenant thereto, hot water heaters plumbing and bathroom fixtures, electric and other lighting fixtures, mantels, outside television antennae, fences, screens, gates, trees, shrubs, plants, and, if built in, air conditioning equipment, ventilators, garbage disposers, and dish-washers and:

9. Title Deed
Said premises to be conveyed by a good and sufficient _____ deed running to the BUYER, or to the nominee designated by the BUYER by written notice to the SELLER at least seven days before the deed is to be delivered as herein provided, and said deed shall convey a good and clear record and marketable title thereto, free from encumbrances, except:
   (a) Provisions of existing building and zoning laws;
   (b) Existing rights and obligations in party walls which are not the subject of written agreement;
   (c) Such taxes for the then current year as are not due and payable on the date of the delivery of such deed;
   (d) Any liens for municipal betterments assessed after the date of this agreement;
   (e) Any easement, restriction, or agreement of record presently in force and applicable which does not interfere with the reasonable use of the premises as now used.

10. Plans
If said deed refers to a plan necessary to be recorded therewith, the SELLER shall deliver such plan with the deed in form adequate for recording or registration.

11. Possession and Condition of the Premises

Full Possession of the Premises, free of all tenants and occupants, except as herein provided, is to be delivered at the time of the delivery of the deed, said Premises to be then (a) in the same condition as they now are, reasonable use and wear and tear thereof excepted, and (b) not in violation of applicable building and zoning laws. The Purchaser shall be entitled to personally inspect said Premises prior to the delivery of the deed in order to determine whether the condition thereof complies with the terms of this section.

12. Extension to Perfect Title or Make Premises Conform

If the Seller shall be unable to give title or to make conveyance or to deliver possession of the premises, all as herein stipulated, or if at the time of the delivery of the deed the Premises do not conform with the provisions hereof, as the case may be, then the Seller shall use reasonable efforts to remove any defects in title, or to deliver possession as provided herein, or to make the said premises conform to the provisions hereof, as the case may be, in which event the time for performance hereunder shall be extended for a period of thirty (30) days; provided however, that "reasonable efforts" herein shall not require Seller to expend more than $2,000, exclusive of voluntary liens.

13. Failure to Perfect Title or Make Premises Conform

At the end of the extended period, if all such defects have not been removed, or the Seller is unable to deliver possession, or the Premises do not conform with the requirements of this Agreement, Buyer may elect to terminate this Agreement and to receive back all deposits, upon receipt of which all obligations of the parties shall cease.

14. BUYER's Election to Accept Title

At the original or extended time for performance, Buyer may elect to proceed with the Closing upon payment of the full Purchase Price reduced by an amount sufficient to remove all mortgages, attachments, and other encumbrances which secure the payment of money which have not been removed by Seller but otherwise without deduction. In the event that the reason the Premises do not conform is damage to the Premises caused by fire or other casualty insured against, and Seller has not restored the Premises to their former condition and Buyer elects to proceed, Seller shall assign all insurance proceeds to Buyer and the Purchase Price shall be reduced by:

a. the amount of any insurance proceeds which a mortgagee has applied to the mortgage debt, less any amounts reasonably expended by Seller for partial renovation;

b. the amount of any insurance proceeds received by Seller; and,

c. any deductible amount under Seller's insurance policy.

15. Acceptance of Deed

The acceptance of a deed by the BUYER or his nominee as the case may be, shall be a full performance in discharge and release of every agreement and obligation herein contained or expressed, except such as are, by the terms hereof, to be performed after the delivery of said deed.

16. Use of Purchase Money to Clear Title

To enable the SELLER to make conveyance as herein provided, the SELLER may, at the time of delivery of the deed, use the purchase money or any portion thereof to clear the title or any or all encumbrances or interests.

17. Insurance

Until the delivery of the deed, the SELLER shall maintain insurance of said premises sufficient to enable the SELLER to be able to perform in accordance with the terms of this agreement. The current insurance on the property is as currently insured. If it is determined that flood insurance is required to enable the BUYER to close, the BUYER agrees to assume responsibility for same.

18. Adjustments

Operating Expenses (if any), water and sewer use charges, fuel charges, and real estate taxes for the then current fiscal year, shall be apportioned as of the day of performance of this agreement and the net amount thereof shall be added to or deducted therefrom, as the case may be, the purchase price payable by the Purchaser at the time of delivery of the deed. In addition, rental payments, if applicable, for the current rental period shall be apportioned if and when collected by either party.

19. Adjustments of Unassessed and Abated Taxes

If the amount of said taxes is not known at the time of the delivery of the deed, they shall be apportioned on the basis of the taxes assessed for the preceding year, with a reapportionment as soon as the new tax rate and valuation can be ascertained; and if the taxes which are to be apportioned shall thereafter be reduced by abatement, the amount of such abatement, less the reasonable cost of obtaining the same, shall be apportioned between the parties, provided that neither party shall be obligated to institute or prosecute proceedings for an abatement unless herein agreed.

20. Broker

The BUYER and SELLER each warrant and represent to the other that neither has engaged the services of a real estate broker for any purpose relating to either the purchase or the sale of the premises. The BUYER and SELLER agree to indemnify and hold the other harmless from any claims as a result of the inaccuracy of BUYER's or SELLER's respective representations and warranties. The provisions of this paragraph shall survive the delivery of the deed.

21. Buyer's Default; Damages

If the BUYER shall fail to fulfill the BUYER's agreements herein, all deposits made hereunder by the BUYER shall be retained by the SELLER as liquidated and exclusive damages for any breach of this agreement by the BUYER.

22. Financing

In order to help finance the acquisition of the property, the BUYER shall apply for a conventional bank or other institutional mortgage loan of ____% of the purchase price at prevailing rates and conditions. If despite the BUYER's diligent efforts, a commitment for such loan cannot be obtained on or before _____, the the BUYER shall have the option of rescinding this agreement by written notice to the SELLER, prior to the expiration of such time, whereupon all deposits made by the BUYER shall be forthwith refunded and this agreement shall become null and void and without recourse to either party. It is further agreed that the BUYER shall provide such reasonable documentation as may be requested by the Seller in support thereof. In no event will the BUYER be deemed to have used diligent efforts to obtain such commitment unless the BUYER submits a complete mortgage loan application conforming to the foregoing provisions on or before _____.

23. Construction of Agreement

This instrument executed in duplicate is to be construed as a Massachusetts contract, is to take effect as a sealed instrument, sets forth the entire contract between the parties, is binding upon and enures to the benefit of the parties hereto and their respective heirs, devisees, executors, administrators, successors and assigns, and may be cancelled, modified or amended only by a written instrument executed by both the SELLER and the BUYER. If two or more persons are named herein as BUYER their obligation hereunder shall be joint and several. The captions and marginal notes are used only as a matter of convenience and are not to be considered a part of this agreement or to be used in determining the intent of the parties to it.

24. Disclosures

BUYER acknowledges receipt of the following required disclosures:

25. Seller's Obligation

SELLER agrees to cooperate with BUYER and the BUYER's Lender's counsel in executing any necessary, reasonable and customary documents as may be required by BUYER's lender including but not limited to FRPTA, Mechanic's lien, UFFI, and Parties in Possession affidavits, as well as any documentation related to the filing of IRS form 1099.

26. BUYER's Inspection (delete inapplicable paragraph)

This agreement is subject to the right of the BUYER to obtain, at his own expense, a premises inspection by consultants of his own choosing within ten (10) days after the execution of this agreement. If the BUYER is not satisfied with the results of such inspection, this agreement may be terminated without legal or equitable recourse to either party by the BUYER at his election, the parties thereby releasing each other from all liability under this agreement, and the deposit shall be returned to the BUYER, provided that the BUYER shall have notified the SELLER in writing, on or before the expiration date herein specified of his intention to so terminate; failure to so notify will not excuse the BUYER from performance hereunder. In the event that BUYER does not elect to have such inspection or to so terminate within ten (10) days the SELLER is hereby released from liability relating to defects in the premises which the BUYER or BUYER's consultant(s) could reasonably have been expected to discover. In the event that this agreement is terminated pursuant to this paragraph then BUYER agrees to provide such documentation as SELLER may reasonably request which may include a copy of the entire report.

Or

The BUYER hereby acknowledges that the BUYER has been provided an opportunity to conduct inspection(s) of the premises by such inspector(s) selected and paid for by the BUYER. Based upon the inspection(s), BUYER agrees to accept the within described Premises in its "AS IS" condition as of the date of this Agreement without any obligation on the part of the SELLER to make any repairs and/or improvements

27. Risk of Loss

The risk of loss or destruction of or damage to said inventory, fixtures, equipment and Premises from any cause whatsoever at all times on or subsequent to the execution of this document but before the recording of the deed or the date and time referenced in closing verification, whichever is earlier, shall be borne by the Seller.

28. Assignment of Warranties

The Seller at the time of the closing shall assign to the Purchaser any warranties, service contracts, or agreements which are in force and effect, if any there be, as to any appliance, fixture, or other equipment or property to be conveyed as herein contemplated.

29. Notices

Any notice or communication required or permitted hereunder shall be sufficiently given if sent by first class mail, postage prepaid:

To Seller at: _____

_____

_____

To Buyer at: _____

_____

_____

30. Acknowledgement

The BUYER acknowledges that he has not relied upon any warranties or representations not incorporated in this Agreement.

In Witness Whereof, the parties have executed this Agreement as of the day and year first above written.

_____
, Seller

_____
, Seller

_____
, Buyer

State of _____
County of _____, SS

On this _____ day of _____, 200__, before me personally appeared _____. to me known to be the person described in and who executed the foregoing instrument and acknowledged that he/she/they executed the same as his/hers/their own free act and deed.

_____
Notary Public
My commission expires:_____

State of _____
County of _____,SS

On this _____ day of _____, 200__, before me personally appeared _____ to me known to be the person described in and who executed the foregoing instrument and acknowledged that he/she/they executed the same as his/her/ their own free act and deed.

_____
Notary Public
My commission expires: _____

State of _____
County of _____,SS

On this _____ day of _____, 200__, before me personally appeared
_____ to me known to be the person described in and who executed the foregoing instrument and acknowledged that he/she/they executed
the same as his/her/ their own free act and deed.

_____

Notary Public
My commission expires: _____

Owner Protection from Post-Closing Claims

Many *by-owner sellers* worry that, without a real estate agent, they will be more vulnerable to claims made by their buyers after the sale. The first thing that you should know is that agents provide little, if any, protection for you. It no longer surprises me to see how fast many agents turn and point the finger to their former customer, the seller, after the seller's home has sold and the buyer initiates some claim. If you live in a state that mandates disclosure of defects to buyers, then the best protection is to be truthful and forthcoming in your disclosure statement. In other states, you have the obligation to respond honestly to direct questions posed to you by the buyer. Beyond these sound policies, you can incorporate some provisions in your *Purchase and Sale Agreement* to serve as additional protection. The following provisions should be reviewed for consideration in adding to your agreement.

Acceptance of the Deed

> *Acceptance of the Deed: The acceptance of a deed by the Buyer or his or her nominee shall be deemed to be a full performance and complete discharge of every obligation herein required by Seller, except for those, if any, explicitly to be performed after the delivery of said deed.*

This provision makes it clear that when the buyer accepts the deed, it legally signifies that he or she acknowledges that the seller has performed the duties that he or she needed to perform and that all of the seller's obligations are extinguished.

Warranties and Representations

> *Warranties and Representations: The Buyer acknowledges that he or she has not been induced to enter into this transaction nor relied upon any warranties or representations not set forth or incorporated in this agreement. This agreement shall represent the sole and exclusive understanding of the parties. The Buyer shall hold the Seller harmless for information available via public record.*

This provision rules out the buyer's ability to later claim that he or she relied on something the seller told or gave to him or her that later proved inaccurate.

It also places the burden on the buyer of finding out any information about the home and area available to the public.

As Is Condition

> *As Is Condition: Buyer has full knowledge of the premises in that Buyer has obtained a home inspection report and is or will be familiar with the condition of same as of the date of the execution of this Agreement. Buyer acknowledges that he or she has relied exclusively on his or her own inspections and his or her right to inspect and the purchase price reflects such rights and the Buyer is purchasing the premises in its "As Is" condition without further recourse to Seller in law or in equity. Seller has not made and does not make any representations as to the physical condition, expense of operation or any other matter or thing affecting or relating to the property or nonexistence of any (i) paint, insulation, plaster, or other accessible substance which contains dangerous amounts of lead or other substances as defined in applicable laws or regulations, (ii) area formaldehyde foam insulation, and (iii) radon.*

This provision helps to turn the fact that your buyer obtained a home inspection into your advantage. It has the buyer state in writing that he or she had the inspection, is aware of its results, negotiated the price of the home after taking into consideration the inspection results, and releases the seller of any possible future claims relating to the home's condition.

If your buyer does not request to undertake a home inspection, you may substitute the following for the first two sentences of the above provision—

> *Buyer acknowledges that he or she has been afforded an opportunity by the Seller to conduct a complete home (termite/pest, radon, lead paint, septic system, water, soil, and structural) inspection and has knowingly and voluntarily waived such inspection. The Buyer, nevertheless, fully acknowledges that he or she is purchasing the premises in its "As Is" condition without further recourse to Seller in law or in equity."*

Disclosures

> *Buyer's Acknowledgement of Receipt of (Lead Paint) Disclosure(s): Buyer acknowledges that he or she has received, read, and signed documents entitled: Disclosure of Information on Lead-Based Paint and/or Lead-Based Paint Hazards.*

Pursuant to federal law, every purchaser of a home built prior to 1978 must be given a standard *Lead Paint Disclosure*. Home built before 1978 may contain lead paint or lead-based materials that can be seriously harmful to small children who ingest flaking paint or particles. Real estate agents generally forward this form to the prospective buyer prior to signing the *Purchase and Sale Agreement*, but as a *for sale by owner* seller, you will have to assume this duty. The form has a few purposes. It:

- ◆ notifies buyers that the home may have lead-based paint and therefore potentially pose a risk to young children;
- ◆ recommends that buyers opt for a 10 day contingency period to conduct a risk assessment or inspection for lead-based hazards in the home prior to purchase ;
- ◆ requires the seller to disclose his or her knowledge of any lead-based paint in the home and to provide the buyer with any and all available reports pertaining to lead hazards in the home; and,
- ◆ requires the buyer to acknowledge receipt of any documents received from the seller as well as the opportunity to conduct the recommended risk assessment or inspection.

A good time for you to have your buyer sign the *Disclosure of Information on Lead-Based Paint and/or Lead-Based Paint Hazards* is when you meet with your buyer to sign the *Purchase and Sale Agreement* and to exchange the deposit. If you have a lead inspection report, a risk assessment report, a letter of interim control, or a letter of compliance, you will need to give copies of these to your buyer. You would have at least one of these documents if you had the home tested for lead paint, and likely would have more or even all of them if you had the home *de-leaded*. You may also have these documents if the prior owner forwarded copies to you at the time of your signing the *Purchase and Sale Agreement*.

If your buyer chooses to conduct the lead-based hazard inspection, he or she would have 10 days (or other agreed upon period) to hire a licensed lead paint inspector and receive the results. If he or she is not satisfied with the results, he or she could opt to cancel the transaction and receive his or her deposit back.

If you are in an area that requires disclosure of known defects, you may want to use this part of the *Purchase and Sale Agreement* to also confirm the buyer's receipt of this disclosure. The acknowledgement of this disclosure will all but eliminate your buyer from later claiming that you failed to provide it.

A sample *Disclosure of Information on Lead-Based Paint and/or Lead-Based Paint Hazards* follows on the next page.

Disclosure of Information on Lead-Based Paint and/or Lead-Based Paint Hazards

Lead Warning Statement

Every purchaser of any interest in residential real property on which a residential dwelling was built prior to 1978 is notified that such property may present exposure to lead from lead-based paint that may place young children at risk of developing lead poisoning. Lead poisoning in young children may produce permanent neurological damage, including learning disabilities, reduced intelligence quotient, behavioral problems, and impaired memory. Lead poisoning also poses a particular risk to pregnant women. The seller of any interest in residential real property is required to provide the buyer with any information on lead-based paint hazards from risk assessments or inspections in the seller's possession and notify the buyer of any known lead-based paint hazards. A risk assessment or inspection for possible lead-based paint hazards is recommended prior to purchase.

Seller's Disclosure

(a) Presence of lead-based paint and/or lead-based paint hazards (check (i) or (ii) below):

   (i) _____ Known lead-based paint and/or lead-based paint hazards are present in the housing (explain).

   _____

   (ii) _____ Seller has no knowledge of lead-based paint and/or lead-based paint hazards in the housing.

(b) Records and reports available to the seller (check (i) or (ii) below):

   (i) _____ Seller has provided the purchaser with all available records and reports pertaining to lead-based paint and/or lead-based paint hazards in the housing (list documents below).

   _____

   (ii) _____ Seller has no reports or records pertaining to lead-based paint and/or lead-based paint hazards in the housing.

Purchaser's Acknowledgment (initial)

(c) _____ Purchaser has received copies of all information listed above.

(d) _____ Purchaser has received the pamphlet *Protect Your Family from Lead in Your Home.*

(e) Purchaser has (check (i) or (ii) below):

   (i) _____ received a 10-day opportunity (or mutually agreed upon period) to conduct a risk assessment or inspection for the presence of lead-based paint and/or lead-based paint hazards; or

   (ii) _____ waived the opportunity to conduct a risk assessment or inspection for the presence of lead-based paint and/or lead-based paint hazards.

Agent's Acknowledgment (initial)

(f) _____ Agent has informed the seller of the seller's obligations under 42 U.S.C. 4852d and is aware of his/her responsibility to ensure compliance.

Certification of Accuracy

The following parties have reviewed the information above and certify, to the best of their knowledge, that the information they have provided is true and accurate.

Seller	Date	Seller	Date
Purchaser	Date	Purchaser	Date
Agent	Date	Agent	Date

Protection From Buyer's Agent's Commission

It can be expected that some prospective buyers will be brought to your home or referred by real estate agents. The agent may be being fully compensated by the buyer or may attempt to negotiate your paying his or her fee out of your sale proceeds. Often you will not know whether a buyer is working with an agent or not. Because of the possibility that the buyer's agent later may make a demand for a fee based on a percentage of your sale proceeds (or an agent may even appear from nowhere at the time of the sale and claim a fee), it is strongly recommended that sellers take precaution. They may do so with language in the *Purchase and Sale Agreement* wherein the buyer *guarantees* that he or she has not worked with an agent in the purchase of your home. The following language is effective:

> *The Buyer represents and warrants to the Seller that the Buyer has not contacted any undisclosed real estate broker in connection with this transaction and was not directed to the Seller as a result of any services of any real estate broker. The Buyer agrees to indemnify the Seller against and hold harmless the Seller from any claim, loss, damage, cost or liability for any brokerage commission or fee that may be asserted against the Seller in connection with this transaction. The provisions of this Paragraph shall survive the deed.*

This provision will place the burden on the buyer to ensure that there is no fee due to an agent. After all, the buyer is the person in the best position to know about the existence of a buyer's agent. It should be noted that if you make this request, the buyer, or his or her attorney, may ask you to make a similar representation—namely that you have not dealt with a broker in this sale and that you will hold the buyer harmless if this proves to be untrue.

Additional Contract Provisions

Invariably, the buyer will propose at least some other provisions to be included in the *Purchase and Sale Agreement*, especially if the buyer is represented by an attorney. Often, these additional provisions will be in the form of a separate *Rider* or *Addendum* that will be referred to in the *Purchase and Sale Agreement* and attached to it.

There are many different types and styles of these provisions. While it is important for you to have your attorney review these specific additions, especially where you do not understand them fully, the following are a brief description of a few of the most common.

Title

A *title* provision, at its most basic level, is the buyer's attempt to rule out any title issues that will not appear from a title examination at the registry of deeds. The buyer is stating that he or she will not be required to buy the home if any part of your home or any of its structures (such as shed, pool, fence, or septic system) is not fully within the boundary lines, if any of your neighbors structures are on your property, if you are not on a public road that the town will service, and if he or she is not able to obtain title insurance at closing.

The inclusion of this language has the effect of inducing the seller to re-review these issues as they relate to this home and disclose and resolve any matters that would put the seller in violation. For example, if you believe that your backyard shed is on your neighbor's property, you may have to move it so as not to jeopardize the sale. Typical language found regarding a title provision would read—

> *Title: Notwithstanding anything herein contained, the premises shall not be considered to be in compliance with the provisions of this Agreement with respect to title, unless:*
> *a. all buildings, structures and improvements, including, but not limited to garages, driveways, septic systems/cesspools and leeching fields, if any, shall be located completely within the boundary lines of said premises and shall not encroach upon or under the property of any other person or entity;*
> *b. no building, structure or improvements of any kind belonging to any other person or entity shall encroach upon or under said premises;*
> *c. the premises shall abut a public way, duly laid out or accepted by such city, town, or municipality; and,*
> *d. title is insurable for the benefit of the Buyer by a title insurance company at normal premium rates in the American Land Title Association form currently in use, subject only*

to those printed exceptions to title normally included in the jacket to such form and to the exceptions set forth in this agreement.

Broom-Clean Condition

This provision is requested by the buyer to avoid an unfortunate yet common occurrence of the seller leaving many of his or her unwanted and worthless items behind for the buyer to deal with. If your buyer requests similar language, make sure that the time deadline specified is something that is not at odds with your schedule. For example, if your movers are not scheduled to come until 10:00 a.m., you will need to make the stated time later. The provision may read something to the effect of—

Broom-Clean Condition: Seller shall deliver the Premises in broom clean condition, free and clear of all of Seller's personal property not included in the Purchase price and all of Seller's trash by 8:00 a.m. on the closing date to allow Buyer to conduct a final inspection of the home.

Right of Access

A *right of access* clause will almost always be included in a *Purchase and Sale Agreement.* It may read—

Right of Access: The Buyer and his or her agents shall have the right of access to the premises prior to the time specified for delivery of the Seller's deed for the purpose of taking measurements or allowing the buyer's bank appraiser to inspect.

Although this may appear to be a reasonable request, it can be quite disruptive, especially to a seller and his or her family who are busy trying to move themselves. In order to strike a happy balance, consider adding the following limiting language—

Said right of access shall be limited to a total of three times and shall only be exercised in the presence of Seller or Seller's designated agent and only after 24-hour notice to Seller.

Sale of Buyer's Home

The *sale of home* contingency is a very powerful provision that protects buyers. Accordingly, while it sometimes is seen in buyer's markets, it is rarely seen in seller's markets. If your buyer requests this term, you should consider it *only* if you believe that your options for selling it to someone else quickly are dismal. If you are in a seller's market or at least in a steady market, and your home is attractive, in a decent area, and reasonably priced, you should not have to accept this term. The provision will read as follows—

> *Contingent on the Sale of Buyer's Home: Buyer's purchase of Seller's home is contingent upon Buyer entering into a Purchase and Sale Agreement with a buyer for Buyer's home on or before _____ (or, is contingent upon buyer closing on his or her home with a buyer on or before _____.)*

This provision can be thought of as a *super financing contingency*. The buyer will be allowed to back out of your deal if he or she cannot obtain a financing commitment from a lender in time or if your buyer does not find a buyer or sell his or her home in time. Therefore, even if your buyer's lender will give the requested loan to buy your home, your buyer, with loan commitment in hand, can still lawfully back out of the deal if he or she does not have his or her home under agreement (or sold) by a certain date. The buyer is putting the risk of selling *his or her* house on *you*.

48-Hour Kick-Out Clause

If you believe you need to accept this term or risk not selling your home for a while, request to add a *48-Hour Kick-Out Clause* to the sale of home contingency. The 48-Hour Kick Out Clause allows you, as of an agreed-upon date, to begin remarketing and reshowing your home again to the buying public. If another buyer comes along and offers to buy your home for a price equal to or greater than the first buyer's offer and without a sale of home contingency, then you can notify your first buyer in writing of this development and he or she will have 48 hours from this notification to choose to either continue with his or her purchase (at the original price) but dropping the *sale of home contingency*, or drop his or her purchase altogether and receive his or her deposit back. The added-on kick out clause tends to be a good compromise for both parties. The standard language for the 48-Hour Kick-Out Clause that you can use in your *Purchase and Sale Agreement* is as follows—

> *This Agreement is contingent upon the Buyer's property locat-ed at [buyer's property address] being under Purchase and Sale Agreement by _____ ____, 200( ) and closing by_____ ____, 200( ). In consideration of the above, the Seller shall have the right to continue to show the home at [seller's property address] to other prospective buyers. If, after [an agreed upon date before closing] the Seller here-under receives an acceptable offer from a third party to buy the real estate as contemplated by this Agreement, then the Seller hereunder shall have the right to accept said offer, pro-vided, however, that the Seller give the buyer hereunder forty-eight (48) hours written notice of his or her intention to accept said alternative offer. Within that forty-eight hour peri-od, the Buyer hereunder shall have the right to delete any contingencies relative to the sale of his or her current home [buyer's property address], and this Purchase and Sale Agreement will continue in full force and effect with no con-tingencies for the sale of [seller's property address]. If, after receiving forty-eight (48) hour notice as contemplated above, the Buyer hereunder does not elect to remove said contin-gency, then the Seller hereunder shall have the right to accept the alternative offer, and all deposits held under this Agreement shall be returned to the Buyer without further recourse to the parties hereto.*

EXECUTING THE PURCHASE AND SALE AGREEMENT

When all the terms and language have been ironed out and a final version has been agreed to by both you and your buyer, its time to sign. At least *two* orig-inal drafts of the *Purchase and Sale Agreement* should be signed so that you and the buyer each have originals. If either party makes a correction or change to any of the provisions, both parties should initial it so that it is clear that the change was made with the knowledge and approval of both parties. Ideally, you should meet and execute the agreements together, so that the buyer can tender his or her deposit check to you simultaneously. If this is not possible, the buyer should sign the multiple copies first and then forward them to you to sign.

The buyer's deposit check is due when you sign the documents in order to make it an enforceable contract. On a multipage *Purchase and Sale Agreement*, it is advisable to have the parties initial each page and then sign the last *signature* page. Also, in order to facilitate the transaction, offer to provide your buyer with an extra copy of the *Purchase and Sale Agreement* for his or her lender. The sooner the lender receives its copy, the faster it can begin work to qualify the buyer for the loan.

SELLING TIPS

If possible, retype any changes made to the Purchase and Sale Agreement into it and then print a new, clean original.

chapter eight:

Preparing for a Smooth Closing

I often tell my clients that, if you arrive at the point where you sit down at the closing, virtually all of the hard work has been done and most of the potential problems have been extinguished. The closing should be, and often is, a pleasant experience for the buyer and the seller. While there are always closing day *horror stories* that attorneys, real estate agents, and escrow agents enjoy telling (and often embellishing further with each new person they tell), the majority of details, decisions, and difficulties, are addressed before this day. In this chapter, the common scenarios that a seller may encounter leading up to the closing are examined and viable solutions that you may employ are discussed.

HOME INSPECTION

Early on in the purchase process, the buyer normally has the ability to conduct an inspection of your home. In areas that use an *Offer* agreement, this occurs after the offer is made and before the *Purchase and Sale Agreement* is signed. In the areas that only use the *Purchase and Sale Agreement*, the inspection takes place within a couple of weeks after this is signed.

The purpose of the inspection is to allow the buyer to have the benefit of an expert looking at the home so that some of the *latent defects*, whether or not known by the seller, may be learned. The buyer often will hire a professional home inspection company to go through the home and all of its structures and mechanical systems. In addition, the buyer may hire additional individuals or companies to also determine the level of radon gas, inspect for termites and other pests, reveal whether there is lead paint, and test the well and/or water purity. The inspectors, in exchange for their fee, generate a report for the buyer advising them of their findings. The buyer, in turn, decides if and how they want to proceed with their purchase.

As discussed in Chapter 7, the *home inspection contingency provision* in most agreements allow the buyer to rescind the offer if he or she:

- ◆ fails the stated test, whether it be the subjective standard or the objective standard and
- ◆ gives proper notice to the seller within the agreed-upon time frame.

More often than not, buyers will approach the seller with some of their inspector's findings. However, it is rare that buyer's pay strict attention to the terms of the inspection contingency, even when buyers are working with agents. Rather, the buyer often will submit a list of items for repair prior to closing. Some buyers, instead, will use the findings to demand that the seller reduce the agreed-upon sales price. In neither of these cases, however, is the buyer complying with the explicit terms of the inspection contingency, and, as the seller, you can use this to your advantage.

Negotiating after the Inspection

A buyer is perfectly free to attempt to request repairs or negotiate the purchase price as a result of the inspection. However, in order for the buyer to keep his or her deposit safe while doing this, he or she must give *proper and timely notice* that he or she wants to *void the deal* and wants his or her *deposit back* as a result of inspection findings. He or she must also state that the inspection findings are either not satisfactory (*subjective standard*) or contain serious structural, mechanical, or other major defects (*objective standard*).

If, without proper and timely notice, the buyer threatens to rescind the offer as a result of the inspection and your failure to give in to his or her demands, you will be able to gently remind him or her that you lawfully can keep the deposit. Demonstrating to the buyer that he or she has not complied with the agreement will give you significant leverage in negotiating the inspection results.

Beyond requiring that the buyer adhere to the strict language of the agreement, there are a few other pointers to keep in mind with inspection contingencies. It is important to recognize that as much as you want to sell your home, your buyer likely wants to buy it at least as much. Buying a home is not an impulse purchase. Therefore, except in extreme buyers' markets, it is not likely that your buyer will walk away if you do not accede to all of his or her demands.

Purchase Price Includes Inspection Findings

Tell the buyer that the purchase price you set for the home took into consideration the items that the home inspector found. It is rare that the buyer will walk away. Usually, this would happen only where the home suffered from such serious structural defects that the buyer was no longer interested in purchasing it—no matter the price.

SELLING TIPS

Although you must weigh the benefits of making the deal work versus the cost of giving concessions to the buyer, feel confident that once the buyer makes an offer on your home, his or her heart has spoken. Your decision to not reduce the price is not likely to change matters.

In some cases, however, the buyer may react personally that you rejected his or her demands and refuse to negotiate the inspection results. He or she consequently may be poised to walk away as a matter of principal. In this case, you may want to weigh your other sale prospects. If they are not great, consider offering only a small portion of what the buyer seeks. As a result of *getting something* coupled with his or her probable great desire for the home, the buyer will likely agree.

Purchase Price Reduction

If you do decide to consent to the buyer's request, only agree to do a *price reduction*. Avoid agreeing to do the repairs requested or to have the repairs done by a contractor. More importantly, do not agree to an escrow arrangement wherein you will have some of your proceeds held back while you or others finish the repairs after the sale. Reducing the price so the buyer can take care of the repairs is your safest bet. If you choose either of the two other alternatives, there is too much subjectivity involved. Your repair work may not match your buyer's conception of how the repair should have been handled. What's worse, if you agree to finish the repairs after you sell the home and have some of your proceeds held in escrow until you do so, you may do all of the work only to have an unsatisfied buyer object to the release of your money.

A reduction of the sale price removes all of this risk and the matter is resolved at closing and not a moment later. Moreover, a reduction in the sale price will reduce the tax you probably will have to pay on the sale and may reduce any capital gains tax. (If you use a broker or have agreed to pay the buyer's broker, their fee will likewise be reduced as well).

BUYER ASKS FOR HELP WITH FINANCING

It is very rare for the buyer to ask the seller to finance the entire sale, but as a *by-owner seller*, you may be approached with this proposition. Here, the buyer asks to be allowed to pay the seller some amount of deposit and then finance the rest by giving the seller a mortgage and making payments over the course of time, probably several years.

Purchase Money Mortgage

This is commonly referred to as a *purchase money mortgage*. This should classify as a *red flag* if ever there was one. Essentially, this is an admission by the buyer that he or she does not qualify for conventional financing through a lending institution.

There are two important problems inherent in financing the entire sale. The first is that, by definition, you will not be able to have the proceeds of your sale in a lump sum payment. Therefore, you will not be able to turn around and use them toward the purchase of another home. The second problem is your lack of relevant experience and skill. As a seller, you are not in the business of lending money and receiving mortgages. You probably are not adept at evaluating another person's credit worthiness. You probably do not have expertise at evaluating tax returns, financial statements, and credit reports.

You probably do not have a legal loan application, note, mortgage (sometimes referred to as a deed of trust), and other necessary lending documents prepared and ready to use at your fingertips. You also probably do not have a collection agency, collections counsel, foreclosure counsel, auctioneer, and bankruptcy counsel on retainer waiting for their next assignment. In short, a seller's financing of the entire purchase is a bad idea.

Second Mortgage

On more frequent occasions, the buyer will ask the seller to take back a *second mortgage*. In other words, the buyer will use his or her own funds to put toward the purchase of the home, will borrow money from and give a first mortgage to a lending institution for a large chunk of the purchase price, and will ask you to loan the balance, and, in turn, give you a *second mortgage*. A buyer generally makes this request if he or she does not qualify for the full amount of the mortgage loan needed to buy your home.

> **Example:** Let's say you and the buyer have agreed to a purchase price of $300,000 for your home. The Buyer is able to put down a total of twenty percent, or $60,000 of his or her own money. He or she then seeks a mortgage from a lending institution for the balance, $240,000. He or she later learns that the bank will only agree to lend $200,000, and therefore he or she will need $40,000 in order to proceed with the purchase. Consequently, he or she approaches you to finance the $40,000 balance.

Unlike the purchase money mortgage, you will only be lending a small portion of the sale price (in our example fifteen percent). Your risk is significantly less.

Evaluating the Risk

In evaluating this risk, the first fact to consider is that at the closing you will not have the amount of the second mortgage that you finance. Therefore, if you were relying on the entire sale proceeds to pay off your current mortgage, pay the sales tax due upon the sale, pay all other closing costs, and use the balance toward the down payment of your next home, the seller financing option is not for you. You will be able to offer this option to your buyer if you:

◆ do not require all of your proceeds immediately to buy your next home;

◆ are moving into an apartment; or,

◆ are selling a rental property.

The second issue to determine is what the *sale prospects* for your home are.

◆ Did I list the home just last week or has it been *sitting* for sale for six months?

◆ Are homes selling rapidly in my area for close to the asking price?

◆ Do I have the luxury of waiting for alternative cash offers to arrive?

◆ Is my home in good condition and in a respectable area such that it will be considered desirable by others?

If by examining these questions you determine that you should not have a problem selling your home and/or you are in no rush, then pass-up the buyer's request. If however these questions cause you to believe that it may be some time before you receive another offer, you should further consider the buyer's request.

The third issue to answer is whether the buyer's lender will allow the buyer to engage in this seller financing. Because your loan to the buyer would entail additional debt and another monthly obligation for the buyer, the bank may explicitly prohibit any secondary seller financing. Moreover, many *Purchase and Sale Agreements*, especially those that are modified by attorneys for buyers, will require that the seller sign at closing those documents that are reasonably required by the lender's attorney. One of these standard documents is an affidavit that both the buyer and seller sign, commonly called a *Fannie Mae Affidavit*, wherein the parties certify that there is no secondary seller-financing. Accordingly, you should request that your buyer provide you with his or her lender's written confirmation that such an arrangement is satisfactory before you move forward. (See Chapter 9 for more information on the *Fannie Mae Affadavit*.)

Acting as a Loan Officer

Beyond this, you will next need to play the role of loan officer and determine how to evaluate the buyer's credit worthiness as well as the terms of the loan that you are willing to offer. First look at how much the buyer is putting down on the transaction. The less of his or her own money he or she puts down, the more risky is the proposition. The more the buyer must pay to the first lender, the less available to pay you.

Ask what terms the buyer wants to give you with the loan. As the seller you want as short of a term for the loan as possible. Five years or less is advisable. The interest rate should be higher than what the buyer could obtain for the same type of loan from a institutional lender. If a lender would require a 6.5 % interest rate for a short term, second mortgage, and your buyer does not qualify, you should require 7.5% or more to compensate you for the service and for your risk. The buyer should have the intent as well as an incentive to refinance as soon as is able.

Next, you will also need to be provided with documents so that you can determine the buyer's ability to repay you. These include:

◆ copies of tax returns for the past three years;

◆ copies of W-2 statements for the last three years; and,

◆ a copy of the buyer's current credit report.

You can obtain the credit report by having your prospective buyer contact one of the three main credit reporting bureaus:

◆ Equifax at **www.equifax.com**;

◆ Experian at **www.experian.com**; and,

◆ Trans Union at **www.transunion.com**.

You should ask your buyer to forward to you a *3 in 1* report which will provide you with a comprehensive report from all three bureaus along with his or her *Fair Isaac credit score*. A Fair Isaac credit score, more commonly referred to as *FICO score*, is the standard used to measure the credit worthiness of individuals. Your buyer can expect to pay about $30.00 to $40.00 for this report.

Additionally, have your buyer complete and sign a basic loan application wherein he or she provides you with other important information such as any co-borrower's name, address, social security number, employer, salary, an itemized list of assets and liabilities, statements regarding creditworthiness, and a signed acknowledgment under the pains and penalties of perjury.

A sample Loan Application follows on the next pages.

LOAN APPLICATION

Borrower's Name	Co-Borrower's Name:
Social Security No:	Social Security No:
Address: Address:	
Telephone No:	Telephone No:
Name and Address of Employer:	Name and Address of Employer:
Title Supervisor:	Title: Supervisor:

Asset Type	Description	Cash or Market Value
Real Estate		
Bank Account		
Bank Account		
Stocks, Bonds, Mutual Funds		
Stocks, Bonds, Mutual Funds		
Automobile		
Automobile		
Other Asset		

Creditor/Liability	Monthly pmt/time left to pay Unpaid Balance
Alimony:	
Child Support:	

For Each of the Following Questions, please check yes or no:

Question	Borrower		Co-Borrower	
	Yes	No	Yes	No
Are you currently a party to a lawsuit?				
Are there any outstanding judgments against you?				
Have you filed bankruptcy in the last 7 years?				
Is any part of your down payment borrowed?				
Do you intend to occupy the premises as your Principal residence?				

I hereby depose and say upon oath that the representations made by me as set forth above are true and correct.

_____   _____

Borrower   Co-Borrower

Dated: Dated

Next, review all of these source documents to see if they are all consistent. For example, the income stated on the W-2s and tax return should be very similar to what your buyer reports on the application. Likewise, the liabilities reported on the application should be similar to those on the credit report. If the buyer overstates income or understates debts, this reveals something about his or her character and should cause you much hesitation. However, if all of the information provided is consistent, look to see what the buyer's *Fair Isaac* (or *Fico*) *credit score* is. This score ranges from 300 to 850. The higher the better. A person will have three separate Fico scores, one for each of the national credit reporting bureaus. Buyers with credit scores of 680 or more are considered to have good credit worthiness. However, your buyer should be in the group with Fico scores of 750 or higher for you to consider extending credit— to be on the safe side.

Using your common sense and your personal experience in *paying the bills*, evaluate whether the buyer will likely have a problem paying you. Determine how much of the buyer's income is used up to pay current expenses and how much will be used to pay you each month. Consult with your attorney or a banker friend for a second opinion. If you conclude that the buyer is credit worthy for your loan, have your attorney draw up the proper note and second mortgage. Make sure the buyer signs it at the closing and that it gets recorded at the registry of deeds (also known as the recorder of deed's office).

BUYER ASKS FOR EXTENSIONS

After the *Purchase and Sale Agreement* is executed, the buyer needs to get working on his or her *mortgage commitment*. The buyer's lender will require a copy of the agreement as part of the buyer's application. By having it, the bank will also know the terms and deadline for the financing contingency. On most occasions, the bank will be able to give the buyer an answer on his or her application prior to the typical 30-day contingency deadline date. If not, the buyer and/or the buyer's attorney likely will contact you and request an extension. When a buyer's attorney or a careful buyer requests this, he or she is likely to send a letter that:

◆ gives notification that the buyer has not received the loan commitment within the financing contingency deadline;

◆ requests therefore that the deal be voided and the buyer's deposit be returned; and,

◆ simultaneously conveys buyer's desire to keep the deal going and requests that seller to therefore sign an enclosed extension for the deadline.

When presented with this request, you have two basic choices: agree to extend the financing contingency deadline or refuse to extend the financing contingency deadline. If you agree, you could allow the buyer additional time to obtain the commitment to make the deal work. However, you could also be holding up the marketing and sale of your home if the buyer ultimately cannot obtain the loan and backs out before the extended deadline. If you refuse to extend the deadline, you force the buyer to make the choice of continuing with the purchase without the ability to back out and keep the buyer's deposit. If the buyer is not willing to take this risk and backs out, you could lose the potential sale if the buyer ultimately could have obtained the loan commitment. However, if the buyer would have never obtained a loan, you gain all that extra time to find a new, qualified buyer.

The buyer, by requesting an extension, is indirectly telling you two things. One is that he or she is still interested in the purchase of your home (or else he or she would have tried to void the deal). The second is that there could be some sort of problem with the buyer obtaining a loan and his or her request for an extension could signify a greater likelihood of the buyer getting denied by the lender. Therefore, if you are willing to grant the request, know that you have the right to negotiate its terms. For example, you may want to reduce the requested 10-day extension to 3 days.

SELLING TIPS

Any agreement should be in writing and labeled as [number] Addendum to the Purchase and Sale Agreement. Have your attorney review the agreement before you sign.

Additionally, you may want to request that the buyer agree in writing to turn over and forfeit some portion of his or her deposit to you in exchange for your granting this additional time.

The rationale is by doing this, you are relieving the buyer of the risk of losing the home and/or the rest of his or her deposit. Instead, you are bearing the risk that he or she can back out at a later date thus adding to the time of finding another buyer. You should be compensated for this risk. If the buyer feels confident that he or she will eventually get the loan and buy your home, then he or she should have no problem with this as the forfeit portion will be duly credited toward the purchase price.

This technique similarly may be used if the buyer asks for an extension for the closing date. However, because the buyer typically will not have any contingencies left just before the original closing date, you can be more aggressive in requesting compensation for the extension. You see, if the buyer does not meet the agreed-upon closing date, barring any added buyer-protective language in the *Purchase and Sale Agreement*, you will have the right to keep his or her deposit. So, because the buyer stands to lose the deposit if he or she cannot close on time, he or she likely will not mind releasing some portion of it to you in exchange for your granting an extension.

BUYER WANTS TO MOVE IN BEFORE CLOSING

There are occasions where your buyer cannot wait until the closing date to move into your home. He or she may be in the process of being transferred to your area because of a job and need to be situated a week or two earlier than the normal bank closing process will allow. Alternatively, for example, your closing may be scheduled for the middle of September, and your buyer wants his or her children to be able to go to their new school when it starts for the year in the beginning of September. In these situations, if your home is vacant or if you can move out earlier than the closing date, your buyer may ask to be allowed to move in before the closing.

If the buyer brings this up <u>after</u> the *Purchase and Sale Agreement* is already signed, then there is little or no reason for you to agree to this request. After all, it does involve some considerable risk on your part. There are questions as to who would be liable for injuries or damages during the preclosing occupancy. There is also the concern that the buyer may not go through with the purchase and not vacate the house. Unless the buyer offers you an excellent financial incentive (a generous daily occupancy rate) and agrees to sign a *Use and Occupancy* agreement (described later in this chapter), it is best to simply refuse the buyer's request if it comes after the *Purchase and Sale Agreement* already is signed.

If the buyer requests this during the purchase and sale negotiations, you will need to weigh the costs of losing the sale with the costs of something going wrong if you allow the request. To help determine the costs of losing the sale, evaluate the market conditions for selling your home. If they are good for you, refuse the buyer's request. Save any potential personal bitter feelings by telling the buyer your attorney informs you that it is too risky and strongly advises against a buyer moving in before the sale. If the buyer likes the home enough, he or she may drop this request and sign the *Purchase and Sale Agreement* without it.

If selling conditions are not favorable for you, then you may have little choice but to allow the buyer to move in before the closing. Although you really cannot protect against the costs of losing the sale, you can take precautions to minimize the costs of something going wrong when the buyer moves in before the closing. You should require the buyer to agree in the *Purchase and Sale Agreement* to execute a *Use and Occupancy Agreement* prior to his or her moving in. The presigned Use and Occupancy Agreement can be attached to, and referenced in the *Purchase and Sale Agreement* so that there is no question as to what the terms will be. Have your attorney review any *Use and Occupancy Agreement* to make sure it complies with your local laws and practices.

A sample *Use and Occupancy Agreement* follows on the next page.

USE AND OCCUPANCY AGREEMENT

AGREEMENT made this _____ day of _____, 200__ by and between _____ of _____ ("Seller") and _____ of _____ ("Buyer") relative to the property known as _____ (the "Property").

WHEREAS Seller is the owner of the Property as has entered into a purchase and sale agreement with Buyer dated _____ to sell him/her the Property;

WHEREAS at the request of Seller, Buyer has agreed to close on the Property later than called for by the Purchase and Sale Agreement; and

WHEREAS Seller will allow Buyer to move into the Property prior to closing but the parties wish to make clear that no tenancy will be thereby established;

NOW THEREFORE, the parties agree as follows:

Buyer will be entitled to use and occupy the Property beginning _____. through _____ which time Buyer will remove his/her personal property and vacate the Property if closing has not occurred.

Upon execution hereof, Buyer will pay Seller $_____ for such use and occupancy.

No tenancy shall be created by this agreement and in the event Buyer fails to remove his/her personal property by the expiration of the applicable period then they will pay Seller the amount of $_____ per additional day of occupancy or any fraction thereof, together with the costs and legal fees associated with any eviction proceeding, and any and all costs associated with removing Buyer's personal possessions. In addition, the Buyer agrees to waive all claims and defenses to any complaint for summary process brought by the Seller to evict the Buyer.

During the use period Buyer shall keep and maintain the Property in good condition and repair and shall commit no waste upon the Property, but shall not alter the Property without the prior written consent of Seller.

Buyer will indemnify and defend Seller for any loss or liability arising out of their use and occupancy of the Property during the period of their use, including any Buyer's guests or invitees. Buyer will insure their personal property located on the Property during the period of use and occupancy.

Buyer will accept the condition of the Property for purposes of the purchase and sale agreement as of the time they assume use and occupancy.

Closing adjustments will be calculated as of _____, the day use and occupancy commenced.

WITNESS our hands and seals this ____ day of _____, 20___

_____   _____
Buyer: Seller:

HANDLING TITLE DEFECTS

Title defects can take dozens of different forms. As the seller, you have the responsibility of clearing the title before the sale can go through. It may be as common and relatively simple as an undischarged mortgage or a missing assignment of a mortgage. It can also be very cumbersome, such as a a prior unrecorded deed, a court judgment and execution, or a forged deed.

In most standard *Purchase and Sale Agreements*, the seller has the automatic right to extend the closing date by a specified amount of time, typically 30 days, in order to try to rectify the title problem. Although this should be enough time to resolve some of the more minor and common defects, the delay could severely disrupt your plans, not to mention your buyer's. If you are under contract to buy your next home immediately after the closing for your home, you will have to do some quick work (and maybe some quick paying too) to appease your seller to agree to a postponement.

One way to avoid this mess is to commission a title examination of your property as soon as you have decided to sell it, or as soon as you accept your buyer's offer. Your attorney can coordinate this process for you. While the cost varies by state, it generally will not cost you more than a few hundred dollars.

Owner's Title Insurance

If you purchased an *owner's title insurance policy* when you purchased the property, the title search need only begin from the date of that policy to the present. In this case, the cost should be less than one hundred dollars. In many states, the seller is responsible for commissioning and paying for the title exam anyway.

If in your state the buyer and/or the buyer's lender or title agent is responsible for ordering and paying for the title examination, you may want to inform your buyer if you have an owner's title insurance policy. Often, the buyer's lender or title agent can use your policy as a start and complete the title search quicker (and cheaper), thereby giving you extra time prior to closing to correct any title defects.

The title defects themselves require the strict attention of your real estate attorney. If you have an owner's title insurance policy and the defect occurred prior to the date of your policy, you and your attorney should submit the claim to the title insurance company. The title insurance company should be able to act on it quickly and forward a *letter of indemnification* to your buyer informing him or her it will be fully responsible for clearing up the defect and will reimburse the buyer for whatever losses suffered as a result of the defect. This should satisfy the buyer and his or her lender's attorney or title agent so that the deal may close.

If you do not have owner's title insurance or the defect occurred after the date of your title insurance policy, then you will have to resolve the problem yourself and with your money.

FINAL WALK-THROUGH

Your *Purchase and Sale Agreement* most likely will allow the buyer to take a last tour/inspection of your home within a couple of days prior to closing. In practice, buyers like to schedule this an hour or two before closing so that they can see the property in the actual state that it will be delivered to them. While the final walk-through is often an exciting time for the buyers, as they once again see their soon-to-be new home, it can get touchy if the home does not appear as expected by the buyer.

Proper preparation for the final walk-through begins just after you have signed the *Purchase and Sale Agreement*. Review the document to see what your obligations are in delivering the home. Determine whether:

◆ the home needs to be broom-clean;
◆ all personal property in the attic, shed, and basement needs to be completely removed;
◆ certain property such as the refrigerator or the children's swing set needs to stay; and,
◆ any repairs to the home need to be made.

The purchase and sale of a home is largely governed by the principals of contract law. The contract, in your case, is the *Purchase and Sale Agreement*. The buyer can only lawfully object at the final walk through if there is a violation of the terms of the agreement. Therefore, after the agreement is signed, make a list of what you need to accomplish and set a manageable schedule for yourself so that you can complete the list prior to closing.

Schedule a Convenient Time

If your buyers ask to do a final walk-through, schedule it only for a time when you will have finished moving out of the home. If your buyer sees it in disarray, he or she is prone to be uneasy. Also, some of the same tips discussed in Chapter 6 regarding showing your home, still apply for the final walk-through. They include:

◆ *remove the pets and children*—Your buyer will appreciate not having to compete for your attention.

◆ *give the home a once-over*—Even if your home is not required to be in a broom-clean condition, you do not want to ruffle the feathers of jittery buyers this late in the game. Your buyers will appreciate being able to move in without cleaning and your gesture will help set the tone for a harmonious closing.

◆ *know your home*—It is at the final walk-through that buyers will have the most detailed and practical questions about living in the home and especially how things in your home function. Be prepared to explain to them the alarm system, the heating and central air controls, the lawn sprinkler system, or anything else that requires instructions.

Dealing with Misunderstandings

If you do have an issue at the walk-through, it probably will be as a result of a difference in understanding or interpretation of what the *Purchase and Sale Agreement* required. Often, misunderstandings center around the nature of the repairs that the seller was required to do prior to the sale. The buyer may have thought that the steps to the deck would have been replaced with similar pressure-treated wood as the rest of the deck, while the seller understood that installing new pine steps were all that he or she needed to do.

> **SOLD**
> **FOR SALE**
>
> **SELLING TIPS**
>
> *Purchase and Sale Agreements* commonly require the seller to deliver the home in substantially the same condition as when the buyer signed the agreement—reasonable wear and tear excepted.

Other times, misunderstandings arise out of an allegation by the buyer that a particular part of the home is now damaged and that it was not when he or she first toured the home and signed the *Purchase and Sale Agreement*.

A buyer (especially a first-time buyer) who already is quite anxious about the process may magnify the scope of the problem in his or her head, and it may be difficult to resolve. If this happens, assure the buyer that this should not dampen this happy day and that it can be resolved. In order that the misunderstanding does not lead to personal bitterness, suggest that the attorney's take care of the issue at closing. If your buyer arrives at closing, there is a much greater chance that the closing will occur.

Moreover, the attorneys likely have handled dozens of similar situations before and will be able to discuss it without the same intense emotions that the parties often possess. If the attorneys cannot sort out the meaning of the contract or if they agree that the seller did not uphold his or her end of the bargain, they may advise their client to agree to hold some of the seller's proceeds in escrow so that the closing may occur and so that the buyer has security that the problem can be resolved. A reduction in sales price may also be the suggested resolution to end the continued involvement between the seller and the buyer and to close the deal.

chapter nine:
The Closing

The *closing* is the last official step in the purchase and sale process. It is where the seller transfers title to the buyer, via the signed deed, in exchange for the purchase price. If you can check all of the items in the below list, then you are ready to close.

❏ You have a signed *Purchase and Sale Agreement.*
❏ Buyer's inspection contingency deadline has passed.
❏ Buyer's financing contingency deadline has passed.
❏ Buyer has his or her financing commitment.
❏ Title examination is done and any defects are resolved.
❏ Buyer's bank gives its approval to close.

NECESSARY CLOSING DOCUMENTS
In preparation for closing, the seller has a few responsibilities to take care of so that the property and the title can be effectively transferred.

New Deed
The *deed* is the document that symbolizes the title to the real estate. It is a common misconception that all you need to do is give your buyer the deed that you now have. This is not true. Instead, a new deed must be drafted that is specific for this transaction. While the style of deeds changes depending on your state and area, all deeds have four common elements.

Names of the Parties

The parties to a deed are the seller, also known as the *grantor*, and the buyer, also known as the *grantee*. It is important that the seller's name on the new deed to the buyer appears the same as the one on the deed when the seller bought the home. If your name has changed, (e.g., you have since married and no longer use your maiden name) the new deed should reflect your new name and the name that you were *formerly known as* on the prior deed. For example, *Carol Jones f/k/a Carol Smith*.

Words of Conveyance

The deed needs to be clear that the seller has the intent to transfer title to the buyer. The words *grant* or *grants* are commonly used. In addition, although not required, the total amount paid for the property (known as the *consideration*) is often recited.

> **Example:** *James Walker for consideration paid of $500,000.00 grants to Margaret Williams...*

Adequate Property Description

It is important that the deed refer to the specific property being transferred. Sometimes the property is described as being a certain diagrammed lot (with all buildings and structures thereon) on a specified plan recorded at the registry of deeds or office of recorder of deeds.

> **Example:** *Shown as Lot 6 on a plan of land entitled 'Plan of Land for Springville Estates' as set forth on Plan number 1234 at the County Registry of Deeds.*

Other times, the property is described by a *metes and bounds description* that sets a starting reference and measures and describes the property's boundaries.

> **Example:** *Northerly by Lot number 10, 200 feet; easterly by Lot number 2, 150 feet; southerly by Pine Street 200 feet, and westerly by Lot number 5, 150 feet.*

Sometimes the deed will use both means of description.

Seller's Signature

The document means nothing unless it is signed by the person conveying title, the seller. Every person that has some ownership interest in the property will need to sign the deed in order to transfer 100% interest to the buyer. Most states require that the seller's signature be *notarized* by a notary public or justice of the peace. Their job is to confirm that it is, in fact, the actual person signing and that he or she is signing freely and voluntarily.

Your attorney is best suited to prepare the new deed and submit it for approval to the bank's attorney or title agent.

A sample *Quitclaim Deed* follows on the next page.

SAMPLE QUITCLAIM DEED

We, Philip Hanna and Mirka Hanna, of Waurika, Jefferson County, Oklahoma

For Consideration Paid and in full consideration of Three Hundred Thousand Dollars and 00/100 ($300,000.00)

Grant to Christopher Ronalds and Debra Ronalds, husband and wife as tenants by the entirety, of 45 Pine Street, Naples, Collier County, Florida

With QUITCLAIM COVENANTS

The land in North Andover, with the buildings thereon, in Naples, Collier County, Florida, shown as Lot 6 on a plan of land entitled "Plan of Land for Springville Estates dated October 18, 1982" as set forth on Plan Number 1234 as the Collier County Registry of Deeds, being further bounded as described as follows:

NORTHERLY:	By Lot number 10, 200 feet;
EASTERLY:	By Lot number 2, 150 feet;
SOUTHERLY:	By Pine Street, 200 feet, and
WESTERLY:	By Lot number 5, 150 feet.

Containing 30,000 square feet, more or less.

For our title, see deed of David and Marianne Venezia dated January 9, 1988 and recorded at Book 5945, Page 129.

Witness our hands and seals this February 25, 2003.

_____   _____

Philip Hanna   Mirka Hanna

STATE OF OKLAHOMA

Jefferson County, ss   February 25, 2003

Then personally appeared the above named Philip Hanna and Mirka Hanna and acknowledged the foregoing instrument to be their free act and deed, before me,

_____

Rene Jeffrey, Notary Public
My Commission Expires: 10/31/09

Mortgage Payoff Information

You will need to provide the buyer's bank attorney or title agent with the information necessary to fully payoff any and all of the lenders who have mortgages on the property you are selling. This information, referred to as *payoff information*, includes the lender's name, address, telephone number, and your account number. As the lender may need your social security number to access the account, the bank attorney or title agent may ask for this. In addition, you may have to provide your signed authorization allowing your lender to release this information.

Condominium-Specific Documents

If you are selling a condominium, you will need to obtain additional, condominium-specific documents for the closing. You will need to provide a *common fees certificate* that is signed by the trustees or, if authorized, the management company. This document will state whether or not there are any back or current common area charges (commonly called *condo fees* or *assessments*) that are due on your account. If so, these must be paid from your sale proceeds so that the new buyer's account starts clean.

The buyer's lender will also require a *certificate of insurance* from the insurance company or agency that provides the *master insurance policy* for the condominium. The name of the your buyer and his or her lender will need to appear on the certificate to evidence their interests as title holder and mortgage holder, respectively.

Some condominium associations require that they have the *right of first refusal* to purchase the condominium unit prior to the owner selling it to a third party. Check your condominium documents for this requirement. If this requirement does apply, chances are though, that the association will waive its right and allow you to sell to your buyer. If so, you will need to bring to the closing, and probably have recorded, the association's waiver of its right of first refusal.

Documentation for Adjustments

Inherent with home ownership are home-related property tax and utility bills. If you are selling a condominium, you also have the additional condominium fee expense. These bills are often paid monthly, quarterly, or semi-annually. Also, if you are selling rental property, you will have rental income that is typically paid by your tenant or tenants monthly. Therefore, it is very typical that on the day of your closing, you will have to determine how to divide these expenses and income. Common purchase and sale language require that the parties *adjust* these at the closing; as of the day of closing. If you have paid your taxes for the current tax period, then you want to ensure the buyer's bank attorney or title agent gives you credit for any and all taxes that you over paid.

> **Example:** If you pay your quarterly tax bill of $1000, and this pays for the period of July 1st through September 30th, and you close on your home on September 1st, you will be due a credit of approximately one-third of what you paid, or $333.00. This same adjustment process will apply for both condominium fees and rental income.

With your electricity, water, and sewer bills, check with your attorney if you are not sure as to your local custom and practice. Often, you will need to inform the provider that you are moving and they will conduct a final reading a day or two prior to the move. You will then need to pay this amount in order to close out your accounts.

If you heat your home with liquid propane or oil, the standard language in the *Purchase and Sale Agreement* will allow you to be reimbursed for whatever value the fuel left in your tank has on the day of closing. Forward to the closing attorney or title agent proof of your payment for all of these adjustments so that you may receive your due credit at closing.

Limited Durable Power of Attorney

For seller's, the closing process can be quite hectic. You have a sizeable pre-closing *to-do* list. You will have to meet and supervise the movers (or move yourself which only further absorbs your time). You have to maneuver around your busy work schedule. You have to plan for someone to assist with the children. You will be happy to know that sellers have a potential solution to help reduce the craziness. You have the option of giving another person, typically your spouse or attorney, a *limited durable power of attorney* to attend the closing in your place so that you may better manage the other tasks on closing/moving day. Your attorney can draft this up and present it to the bank attorney or title agent for approval a week or so prior to the closing. While this document will allow your designated person to sign all the documents at the closing, you likely will be required to personally sign the deed before hand.

State Specific Requirements

Each state or even area within a state may have its own laws, regulations, or practices as to additional requirements that need to be done by the seller prior to closing. Some states require that a seller obtain a certification by the local fire department that the home has properly placed smoke detectors and that they are properly functioning. Other states, such as Massachusetts, require that a seller, whose home is not connected to public sewer, have the septic system inspected to ensure that it does not affect the ground water. Your attorney will advise you as to the specifics for your area. Make sure you ask about this at your initial meeting so that you have time to comply.

AT THE CLOSING TABLE

The closing is the conclusion of the *Purchase and Sale Agreement*. There are two principal types of closings. Depending on the state and area in which you live, you will either have a *title company/escrow* closing or you will have a *closing attorney/conference table closing*. While both types each result in the deed being transferred by the seller to the buyer in exchange for the purchase price, the methods slightly differ.

The Closing Attorney/Conference Table Closing

This type of closing is coordinated by a lawyer's office that represents the buyer's lender. The closing attorney is charged with the following tasks:

- ◆ to perform a title examination of the property to confirm that there are no defects;
- ◆ to hold the buyer's deposit and loan proceeds along with the seller's deed aside (*in escrow*) pending final resolution;
- ◆ to record the deed and the mortgage at the county recorder (or registry of deeds);
- ◆ to make disbursements to the applicable parties including the seller and the seller's mortgage holder and to pay all sales taxes and other fees; and,
- ◆ to issue a title insurance policy to the lender (and, a separate one to the buyer, if purchased), protecting it from any defects in the title henceforth.

Once the bank advises that the buyer's loan is *OK to close*, the attorney's office contacts the buyer and seller and their attorneys to schedule the closing. The closing is scheduled for the date agreed to by the parties in the *Purchase and Sale Agreement*. The parties meet together and sit down at a conference table at a designated place (usually the bank attorney's office or the registry of deeds). At that meeting, all of the documents are signed by both parties, the deed is signed and given to the bank attorney to record, and the seller's proceeds are held pending the recording.

The Title Company/Escrow Closing

This type of closing is coordinated by a *title company*. A title company is an organization whose principle function is to conduct real estate closings. There is no requirement that the persons conducting the closing be attorneys. The title company is selected by the buyer's lender to handle the same tasks as the closing attorney stated above. In this type of closing however, the buyer and seller rarely meet each other. Instead, when the buyer's bank has approved the loan, the bank will forward the closing documents to the title company, which acts as the *escrow holder*. The title company will then coordinate with the buyer for signing all loan documents ahead of the closing date. Next, the seller will sign and deliver the deed to the title company. The buyer will then pay any additional money needed to close to the title company. The title company then records the necessary documents at the recorder's office, including but not limited to the deed and mortgage, and makes all necessary disbursements including paying the proceeds of the sale to the seller.

Documents Signed at Closing

Despite the variations in the two types of closings, the documents signed by the seller are essentially the same. The important documents you can expect to sign at closing will consist of the following.

Settlement Statement

The settlement statement is commonly referred to as the *HUD*, a nickname derived from the federal agency that mandates its use, the *Department of Housing and Urban Development*. It is an itemization of all of the seller's and buyer's credits and debits for the closing. It was mandated into use in order to prohibit undisclosed fees and settlement charges.

The first page of the settlement statement contains the pertinent descriptive information for the closing, including the parties' names and address, the lender's name and address, the property location, the settlement agent's name and address, and the closing (or settlement) date. The remainder of the two-page settlement statement is divided into two columns. The left column of both pages is the *buyer's side* and the right column of each page is the *seller's side*.

The top section on the seller's side of the first page (the 400-block) contains the seller's credits. The contract purchase price of the home will appear in line 401 followed by any other credits, such as personal property that the buyer is purchasing in conjunction with the sale and any tax, fuel, or condominium fee adjustments that the buyer owes the seller. The first section on the buyer's side of the first page (the 100-block) contains the debits for the buyer. Such items as the contract purchase price, the sum total of the closing costs, and any adjustments that the buyer owes the seller appear in this section.

The second portion of the seller's front page (the 500-block) contains the seller's debits. This section includes the sum total of the seller's settlement charges, the balance due to any mortgage holders (commonly referred to as the *payoff amount*), the deposit that the seller or his or her attorney is already holding, and any fees, such as taxes, condominium fees, and utility bills, that the seller has not paid and for which he or she needs to reimburse the buyer.

The buyer's credits appear in the 200-block on the bottom of the buyer's side of the first page. The buyer's credits include any deposit he or she has already paid, the amount of the new mortgage loans he or she is receiving, and any monies he or she is receiving from the seller via adjustments for any unpaid taxes, condominium fees, utility bills, or the like.

To find out the net amount that the seller will receive after the closing, the total of the seller's 400-block is reduced by the total of the 500-block. The buyer, similarly, will be required to bring in a check for the difference between the total of the 100-block and the total of the 200-block.

The second page is simply an itemization of all of the settlement costs for each party. The totals of these columns have already been included as debits, as they appear at lines 103 and 502 for the buyer and seller, respectively. The buyer's second page column typically contains many more entries than the seller as the buyer has bank related charges. For the seller, common settlement costs include the recording fee for any mortgage discharges and tax on the sale of the home. Depending on your state, you may have to pay the title exam expense. However, in some states, the buyer will share with you the sales tax expense. Other fees may be charged to you by the attorney or title agent. You should consult with your attorney to determine if any additional charges are customary in your area.

A sample *Settlement Sheet* follows on the next two pages.

F.2853-01 R7/87

OMB No.2502-0265   Page 1

A.

B.TYPE OF LOAN

1. ☐ FHA	2. ☐ FMHA	3. ☒ CONV.UNINS.
4. ☐ VA	5. ☐ CONV.INS.	

6.File Number:
SAMPLE1

7. Loan Number

SETTLEMENT STATEMENT
U.S. DEPARTMENT OF HOUSING AND URBAN DEVELOPMENT

8.Mortgage Insurance Case Number:

C. NOTE *This form is furnished to give you a statement of actual settlement costs. Amounts paid to and by the settlement agent are shown. Lines marked "(poc)" were paid outside the closing; they are shown here for informational purpose and are not included in the totals. WARNING: It is a crime to knowingly make false statements to the United States on this or any other similar form. Penalties upon conviction can include a fine and imprisonment. For details see: Title 18U.S. Code Section 1001 and Section 1010.*
PREVIOUS EDITION IS OBSOLETE.

D.NAME OF BORROWER: Christopher Ronalds & Debra Ronalds
ADDRESS: 45 Pine Street
Naples, Florida

E.NAME OF SELLER: Philip Hanna & Hanna Mirka
ADDRESS: 25 Main Street
Waurika, Oklahoma

F.NAME OF LENDER: Bank of Florida
ADDRESS: 1 Sunset Drive
Naples, Florida

G.PROPERTY LOCATION: 45 Pine Street
Naples, Florida
Collier County

H.SETTLEMENT AGENT:
ADDRESS:

I.SETTLEMENT DATE:
Tuesday
February 25th 2003

PLACE OF SETTLEMENT: Bernard Settlement Services
ADDRESS: Naples, Florida
Collier County

J.SUMMARY OF BORROWER'S TRANSACTION		K.SUMMARY OF SELLER'S TRANSACTION	
100.GROSS AMOUNT DUE FROM BORROWER		**400.GROSS AMOUNT DUE TO SELLER**	
101.Contract sales price	300,000.00	401.Contract sales price	300,000.00
102.Personal property		402.Personal property	
103.Settlement charges to borrower(line 1400)	5,330.12	403.	
104.		404.	
105.		405.	
Adjustments for items paid by seller in advance		**Adjustments for items paid by seller in advance**	
106. City/town taxes 02/25/03 to 03/31/03	372.60	406.City/town taxes 02/25/03 to 03/31/03	372.60
107. County taxes to		407. County taxes to	
108. Assessments to		408. Assessments to	
109.		409.	
110.		410.	
111.		411.	
112.		412.	
120. GROSS AMOUNT DUE FROM BORROWER	305,702.72	**420. GROSS AMOUNT DUE SELLER**	300,372.60
200. AMOUNTS PAID ON BEHALF OF BORROWER		**500. REDUCTIONS IN AMOUNT DUE TO SELLER:**	
201. Deposits or earnest money	15,000.00	501. Excess deposit (see instructions)	
202. Principal amount of new loan(s)	200,000.00	502. Settlement charges to seller (line 1400)	970.00
203. Existing loan(s) taken subject to		503. Existing loan(s) taken subject to	
204.		504. Payoff of first mortgage loan National Bank	58,790.00
205.		505. Payoff of second mortgage loan	
206.		506. Attorney Joseph Carol	750.00
207.		507.	
208.		508.	
209.		509.	
Adjustments for items unpaid by seller		**Adjustments for items unpaid by seller**	
210. City/town taxes to		510. City/town taxes to	
211. County taxes to		511. County taxes to	
212. Assessments to		512. Assessments to	
213.		513.	
214.		514.	
215.		515.	
216.		516.	
217.		517.	
218.		518.	
219.		519.	
220. TOTAL PAID BY/FOR BORROWER	215,000.00	**520.TOTAL REDUCTIONS AMOUNT DUE SELLER**	60,510.00
300. CASH AT SETTLEMENT FROM/TO BORROWER		**600. CASH AT SETTLEMENT TO/FROM SELLER**	
301. Gross amount due from borrower(line 120)	305,702.72	601.Gross amount due to seller(line 420)	300,372.60
302. Less amount paid by/for borrower(line 220)	(215,000.00)	602. Less reductions in amount due seller(line 520)	(60,510.00)
303.CASH(☒ FROM) (☐ TO) BORROWER	90,702.72	**603. CASH (☐ FROM) (☒ TO) SELLER**	239,862.60

PROFESSIONAL DOCUMENT SYSTEMS INC. (603) 437-1541

HUD-1
RESPA HB 4305.2

F.2853-01 R7/87   OMB No.2502-0265   Page 2

L. SETTLEMENT CHARGES

		PAID FROM BORROWER'S FUNDS AT SETTLEMENT	PAID FROM SELLER'S FUNDS AT SETTLEMENT
700. TOTAL SALES/BROKER'S COMMISSION based on price $ @ % =			
Division of commission (line 700) as follows: 300,000.00 0.00000 0.00			
701. $ to			
702. $ to			
703. Commission paid at Settlement			
704.			
800. ITEMS PAYABLE IN CONNECTION WITH LOAN			
801. Loan Origination Fee % Bank of Florida			
802. Loan Discount % Bank of Florida			
803. Appraisal Fee to Nickmar Appraisals		300.00	
804. Credit Report Lucille Credit Services		30.00	
805. Lender's Inspection Fee			
806. Mortgage Insurance Fee			
807. Assumption Fee			
808. Administrative Fee to Bank of Florida		250.00	
809. Application Fee to Bank of Florida		350.00	
810. Processing Fee to Bank of Florida		375.00	
811. Document Prep to Salerno Doc., Inc.		45.00	
812.			
813.			
814.			
815.			
816.			
817.			
900. ITEMS REQUIRED BY LENDER TO BE PAID IN ADVANCE			
901. Interest from 02/25/03 to 02/28/03 @$ 26.9000 /day		107.60	
902. Mortgage Insurance Premium for months to			
903. Hazard Insurance Premium for 1 years to Millie Insurance		525.00	
904. years to			
905.			
1000. RESERVES DEPOSITED WITH LENDER			
1001. Hazard Insurance 2 month @ $ 43.75 per month		87.50	
1002. Mortgage insurance month @ $ per month			
1003. City property taxes month @ $ per month			
1004. County property taxes 3 month @ $ 333.34 per month		1,000.02	
1005. Annual assessments month @ $ per month			
1006. month @ $ per month			
1007. month @ $ per month			
1008.		0.00	
1009.			
1100. TITLE CHARGES			
1101. Settlement or closing fee to Bernard Settlement Services		550.00	
1102. Abstract or title search to Verschuuren Title		160.00	
1103. Title examination to			
1104. Title insurance binder to			
1105. Document preparation to			
1106. Notary fees to			
1107. Attorney's fees to			
(includes above items numbers;			
1108. Title insurance to Nelson Title Guaranty		1,150.00	
(includes above item numbers;			
1109. Lender's coverage $ 550.00 (200,000.00)			
1110. Owner's coverage $ 600.00 (300,000.00)			
1111.			
1112.			
1113.			
1200. GOVERNMENT RECORDING AND TRANSFER CHARGES			
1201. Recording fees: Deed $ 100.00 ;Mortgage $ 125.00 ; Release $ 50.00		225.00	50.00
1202. City/county tax stamps: Deed $ 920.00 ; Mortgage $			920.00
1203. State tax stamps: Deed $; Mortgage $			
1204. Overnight package to National Bank		20.00	
1205. Overnight package to Bank of Florida		30.00	
1300. ADDITIONAL SETTLEMENT CHARGES			
1301. Survey to James Survey		125.00	
1302. Pest inspection to			
1303.			
1304.			
1305.			
1306.			
1307.			
1308.			
1309.			
1310.			
1400. TOTAL SETTLEMENT CHARGES (enter on lines 103, Section J and 502, Section K)		5,330.12	970.00

Borrower_____ Seller_____

Borrower_____ Seller_____

PROFESSIONAL DOCUMENT SYSTEMS INC. (603) 437-1541   HUD-1
RESPA HB 4305.2

Mechanic's Lien Certificate

The buyer's bank attorney or title agent will need to obtain some information from you to issue a title insurance policy to the lender and/or the buyer. You will be asked to sign a *Mechanic's Lien Certificate* wherein you state under oath:

◆ whether or not there are any tenants having rights in the property and

◆ whether you have knowledge of any work having been done to the property for which money is owed such that the person could claim a lien on the property.

If you sign this affidavit, also known as the *Mechanic's Lien Affidavit* or the *Homeowner's Affidavit*, and answer each part in the negative, and it turns out that you knew one or both of your statements were untrue, you may be liable to the settlement agent or the title insurance company for the actual damages incurred. Therefore, report to the settlement agent and note on the *Mechanic's Lien Certificate* any reasons why you cannot answer the statements in the affirmative.

Fannie Mae Affidavit

The *Fannie Mae Affidavit* is a document that contains several representations that the buyer and seller need to swear under oath as being true. The seller is required to affirm that:

◆ to the best of seller's knowledge, information, and belief, the buyer is the same person as the one signing the note and the mortgage for the purchase of seller's home (Representation number 1);

◆ he or she is the seller of the property and is selling to the buyer (Representation number 2);

◆ to the best of seller's knowledge, information, and belief, the purpose of buyer's loan is for the purchase of seller's home (Representation number 3);

SELLING TIPS

Since most lenders will commit to give the buyer a loan only if there is no secondary financing, if you are giving the buyer a second mortgage, you may jeopardize your sale if you answer the Fannie Mae Affidavit honestly. Moreover, if you falsely report that there is no secondary financing, then you have lied in an sworn affidavit which constitutes perjury. Therefore, if you want to offer a second mortgage, have your buyer ask his or her lender to grant its consent to you in writing.

◆ to the best of seller's knowledge, information, and belief, the buyer is not obtaining subordinate financing for the purchase of seller's home (Representation number 4);

◆ to the best of seller's knowledge, information, and belief, the buyer has not given anyone a lien on the property in conjunction with the buyer obtaining subordinate financing (Representation number 5);

◆ unless specifically stated in the affidavit, he or she is not paying for any of the buyer's costs in purchasing the home (Representation number 6); and,

◆ if applicable, to the best of seller's knowledge, information, and belief buyer either already occupies the seller's home or intends to do so within thirty (30) days (Representation 7).

chapter ten:
The Move

One of the most dreadful parts of selling your home is having to pack all of the belongings that you have accumulated, transport them, unpack them, and put them into their new places. In addition, there are the moving dilemmas.

- ◆ Do I rent a truck and try to complete the move myself or do I spend the money and hire a moving company?
- ◆ If I hire a moving company, how do I select one?
- ◆ Do I do the packing myself, or do I let them do it?
- ◆ Is insurance available for the move and should I purchase it?
- ◆ If I do the packing, where do I find boxes?

The following are some moving company-recommended and client-tested suggestions to help keep your moving day…moving.

TIMING YOUR MOVE

The moving business closely tracks the home purchase and sale business. Therefore, it stands to reason that the end of the month (especially between April and October, and especially on a Friday) is by far the busiest time for both moving companies and truck rental companies. This makes it the worst time for you.

If you are looking to book a company or a truck during the last week of the month, you may run out of luck if you do not call at least a month and one-half in advance. If you are lucky enough to secure a reservation, you are significantly more likely to encounter one or more of the following:

◆ smaller selection of trucks, equipment, and supplies;

◆ the late arrival or even non-arrival of the truck and crew;

◆ less number of crew members than requested;

◆ less than normal experienced crew members; and,

◆ generally poorer overall service.

The resolution to this is the same one suggested for scheduling your closing—avoid the end of the month.

AVOID BACK-TO-BACK CLOSINGS AND MOVING

The most logistically difficult task for a seller to coordinate is the sale, purchase, and move all in one day—especially where the buyer of your old home and/or the seller of your new home are also closing and/or moving on the same day. There is no clean-cut way to safely plan for this. There are too many variables (the settlement agent, the other party and his or her attorney, the lender, the registry or recorder of deeds, the mover, and mother nature) that make failsafe planning difficult, if not impractical. Instead, when the two closings and the move are successfully accomplished, it usually can only be attributed to luck. If you must sell your home and buy your next home both in the same day, consider one of the following moving options.

Storage Units

During the few weeks prior to closing, pack and move most of your belongings yourself into a storage facility. This way when your closing day comes, you will not need to move any boxes—only furniture. As boxes often outnumber furniture pieces ten to one, you will be able to move several times faster and thereby free up valuable time (and moving costs) on this busy day. As you move into your new home, the boxes can be retrieved from the storage facility as you need them.

Move Belongings into New Home prior to Closing

Arrange to move your belongings into your next home prior to the closing if possible. More often than you may think, the seller of your next home has vacated prior to the closing. This makes for a great alternative to moving on closing day. Approach your seller and request that you be able to store your possessions in the home a few days prior to closing. If your seller is hesitant, you can offer to sign an *Indemnification Agreement* that will have you assume any risk inherent in the process.

A sample *Indemnification Agreement* for storage follows on the next page.

INDEMNIFICATION AGREEMENT FOR STORAGE

With respect to the property known and numbered _____ ("Premises"), _____ (the "Seller") hereby grant the right to _____ (the "Buyer") to move belongings into the Premises from _____ until the time the deed into them is recorded and funds are released, at which time they will have the right to take occupancy. In exchange for this right:

Buyer agrees to indemnify and hold the Seller harmless of and from any and all clams, actions, causes of action, or any liability whatsoever arising out of Buyer's use and occupancy of the Premises during the term hereof.

Buyer understands, acknowledges and agrees that Buyer's personal property located or placed in the premises during the occupancy period shall be at Buyer's sole risk and hazard, and if any loss or damage occurs, no part thereof whatsoever is to be charged or borne by Seller.

Buyer shall pay Seller the sum of $_____ due at closing for such use and occupancy for storage.

_____   _____

Buyer   Seller

STATE of _____

_____, SS   Date: _____

Then personally appeared before me, _____,
to me personally known and acknowledge their foregoing signatures as their free act and deed, before me

_____

Notary Public
My Commission Expires:

Move after Closing

Ask your buyer to allow you to remain and move out of your home the day after the closing. Frequently, your buyer does not have plans to move into the home until a few days or even longer after the closing. Perhaps the buyer is renting and plans to only move into the home in stages while he or she updates and remodels it. In this case, your buyer should be amenable to your staying in the home one additional night and moving out the next day. Again, you can offer to sign an *indemnification agreement* that will make you fully responsible if you damage the home after the deed is transferred.

A sample *Indemnification Agreement to Remain in the Premises* follows on the next page.

INDEMNIFICATION AGREEMENT TO REMAIN IN THE PREMISES

AGREEMENT made this _____ day of _____ 200__ by and between _____ of _____ ("Seller") and _____ of _____ ("Buyer") relative to the property known as _____, (the "Property").

WHEREAS Seller is the owner of the Property and has entered into a purchase and sale agreement, as amended, with Buyer dated _____ to sell Buyer the Property on _____;

WHEREAS Seller wishes to remain in occupation of the premises through _____; and

WHEREAS Buyer will allow Seller to remain into the Property subsequent to the closing through _____ but the parties wish to make clear that no tenancy will be thereby established;

NOW THEREFORE, the parties agree as follows:

After the closing scheduled to occur on or about _____, Seller will be entitled to use and occupy the Property through _____ at or before which time Seller will remove his personal property and vacate the Property.

No tenancy shall be created by this agreement and in the event Seller fails to vacate and/or remove their personal property by the expiration of the applicable period, then Seller will pay the costs and legal fees associated with any proceeding brought by Buyer, and any and all costs associated with removing Seller's personal possessions.

During the use period Seller shall keep and maintain the Property in good condition and repair and shall commit no waste upon the Property, and shall not alter the Property without the prior written consent of Buyer.

Seller will indemnify and defend Buyer for any loss or liability arising out of their use and occupancy of the Property during the period of their use, including any Seller's guests or invitees.

Closing adjustments will be calculated as of _____.

Seller, joint and severally, shall be responsible for any costs and reasonable attorney's fees incurred by Buyer relating to the enforcement of this agreement.

WITNESS our hands and seals this _____ day of _____, 20__

_____   _____
Buyer: Seller:

HIRING A MOVER

Unlike an auto mechanic, an accountant, or primary care physician, the moving company is not the type of business people patronize on a frequent basis. Many sellers in need of a mover have never hired one before. Consequently, many tend to first turn to the local telephone book and call a few companies and select the one that quotes the lowest price. This, unfortunately, is a poor choice. There are many low cost movers who undercut the competition by hiring unemployed people who are looking for a day's work, but who are inexperienced in moving. Instead, obtain a referral from someone you trust who interacts with movers. Examples include your real estate attorney, a homebuilder, your banker or mortgage lender, a real estate agent, or someone who has moved recently. Most states license and regulate moving companies so, after you receive your referral, you may want to confirm with the applicable state office their *good standing* status.

Rid Yourself of Unused Items

Most people accumulate more *stuff* than they ever will use or need. Often people are afraid to throw out things because we may have a need for them in the future. However, chances are if you have not worn that brown polyester leisure suit since the 70's or have not used that vintage Apple computer since President Reagan was in office, it will be OK if you throw them out. In the weeks leading up to the closing, have a yard sale, buy a dumpster and fill it up, or make a donation to charity. The general rule of thumb is if you have not worn it, used it, or looked at it in the last two years, get rid of it. Its cheaper to remove it now, than move it on moving day.

Pack Yourself

If you hire movers, do not let them pack for you. Movers pack very carefully. Because they do not know what is valuable and what is not, they must treat everything with great caution. This means that they will spend a lot of time in bubble wrapping inexpensive or even undesirable items. Because movers charge by the hour, this is not a very efficient or cost-effective approach.

Moreover, movers do not know your new home. They are forced to box items according to where they are located in your current home. You, however, by packing yourself, will be able to be more flexible and box and mark items according to where they will go in the new home. This will make your unpacking much more efficient.

SELLING TIPS

The Internet is a good source for boxes and packing supplies. Enter "moving boxes" and "supplies" into your search engine.

Pack all of your essential items into one or two boxes and keep these with you (and not the movers) during your transition. Things you may want to pack in these boxes include: a gallon of water, snacks, paper plates, cups, utensils, napkins, a first aid kit, a hammer and screwdrivers, a flashlight, paper towels, and, if applicable, baby food, diapers, and supplies. Also, keep your jewelry and important closing and financial records in a locked box or suitcase with you.

Prepare for the Movers

Many sellers are not prepared for the arrival of their movers and, consequently, end up paying more money than they needed to pay. Make sure the movers have easy access to your home and doors. If you do not have a driveway, clear three or four on-street parking spaces in front of your home so the moving truck can comfortably park leaving enough room for the crew to maneuver. If there is snow on the ground, make a clean pathway from the truck to your home's door. Disconnect your gas stove and washer and dryer yourself. Also, break down any gym equipment, swing set, and bedroom sets.

Purchase Mover's Liability Insurance

When you engage the services of a mover, the mover will have some responsibility if it loses or damages your goods. The level of its liability depends on which of the four liability options you choose. The provisions of the four options generally have the following terms.

Basic Value Protection

Option 1 (also called *Option A*) is *basic value protection*. It does not cost the customer any money. The mover's maximum liability is generally $0.60 per pound per lost or damaged item. Therefore, if an entire shipment of your property is lost and it weighed, for example, 10,000 pounds, the mover would have to pay you 10,000 lbs. x $0.60 = $6,000, regardless of the actual value of the lost goods.

Depreciated Value Protection

Option 2 (also referred to as *Option B*), is the *depreciated value protection* option. If you select this choice, the mover will either repair the damaged articles to your satisfaction or pay you the value of the item less depreciation. If the whole load is lost, the mover will pay you up to $2.00 for each pound of the total weight. The customer with a $10,000 pound load would receive $20,000. This option is not free and will generally cost between $0.0102 and $0.017 times the total weight of your belongings. So, this option for the 10,000 pound load will cost between $102 and $170. (This option is the default option if you fail to choose one.)

Replacement Cost

Option 3 (also referred to as *Option C*) covers you for the *replacement cost less a deductible*. This is the best option if the entire shipment is lost as you will be entitled to either the full declared value less a $300 deductible or $3.50 times the weight of your total shipment, whichever is greater. However, if one or two items are damaged, the mover will try to repair the damage to your satisfaction. If the mover cannot repair the item, then a $300 deductible will apply, which likely will be more than the value of the damaged item. This option will generally cost you between $0.0044 and $0.0073 x ($3.50 x the total shipment weight). For the 10,000 pound load, you will pay between $154 and $255.50.

Full Replacement Cost

The final option, *Option 4* (also referred to as *Option D*) is the *full replacement cost with no deductible* option. It is the same as Option 3, except you do not have any deductible. The mover will repair any damage to your satisfaction or reimburse you for the full replacement cost. This option will cost you between $0.0062 and $0.0103 x ($3.50 x the total shipment weight). If an entire 10,000 pound load is lost, you will receive the declared value or $35,000, whichever is higher.

Given these choices, consider choosing Options 3 or 4 where your risk of losing the shipment or having it damaged is greater, such as if you are storing your property with the mover over one or more nights or if you are making a long distance move. If you have many individual items of high value such as crystal collectibles or china, choose between Options 2 and 4.

Option 1 only considers the weight, not value, and Option 3 has a $300 deductible that eats up most or all of the replacement cost. If you are making a same day, short move, do not have many stairs in your current or new home, will be following the truck yourself, and do not have many valuable or are holding onto them yourself, then Option 1 may be your best choice.

chapter eleven:
Dealing with the Hard-to-Sell Home

It can be very frustrating for a seller when a home sits for a while without selling. This chapter looks at the main obstacles to a quick and successful sale and provides suggestions to either avoid or overcome them. Also, for those whose homes take longer than envisioned to sell and who no longer have the time or will to sell the home themselves, this chapter will examine how to best select and hire a real estate broker to take over.

REASONS A HOME DOES NOT SELL QUICKLY

Sometimes, despite the seller's efforts, the home, nonetheless, fails to sell. This is not a phenomenon linked solely to *for sale by owner sellers*. Many professional real estate agents, including very successful ones, experience homes that *sit*. What you need to know is that this does not happen without a reason, and you, as the seller, have the ability to remedy the situation. The following is a breakdown of the four basic reasons of what makes homes difficult to sell. Your home may fall squarely into one of these categories or, instead, may fall into two or more, or even all of the categories. Figuring out which category or categories apply to your situation is the first step to turning things around.

Market Conditions

In one respect, the sale of a home is no different than the sale of any other consumer product—it is subject to market forces. Supply, demand, price, quality, and the general economic conditions all shape the prospects for each sale. If there is an over supply of homes on the market in your area and/or there is a low demand for homes, you are in a classic *buyer's market*. When in a buyer's market, it is very important to sell your current home first before you look to buy. If not, you can expect to carry the costs of two homes for a while. The good thing about a buyer's market is if you can successfully sell your home, then you will be able to take advantage of the market for your purchase. However, if you are not looking to buy your next home (you will be moving into an apartment or the home you are selling is investment property), then you really should think twice about selling during a buyer's market.

As the expression goes, *everything has its price*, and price is extremely important in a buyer's market. This is because the buyer has so many choices. Only the attractively-priced homes sell in difficult economic times. As a for sale *by owner seller*, you possess a great advantage. In a neighborhood with five other similarly-styled and priced homes for sale but which are, instead, all using real estate agents. You will be able to lower your price considerably and still pocket more money than the other owners. Exploit this *low overhead* advantage and aggressively price your home for a quick and successful sale.

Home in Poor Condition

Not every home is a showplace. Many have outdated styles and features. Others have roofs or mechanical systems that are in need of serious repair or replacement. These homes do not show well and may consequently sit longer than you would want. If you have a *fixer-upper*, feature the lot layout, the location, or the underlying quality construction of the home in your marketing. The home can be updated, and once it is, the buyer also will have a desirable lot and/or location. Often, older homes, even though in need of rehabilitation, have desirable features such as crown molding, hardwood floors, high ceilings, and solid panel doors that are not widely seen in newer homes. Contact several investors, tradesmen, and builders in your area to see if they are interested. They will have the skill to rehabilitate the home and should be eager to talk with you because, without a broker, you can be more flexible with the price. If the home is in poor enough condition, a builder-buyer may consider knocking it down and building a new home.

Undesirable Location

All else being equal, homes in less desirable locations sell less quickly. Your home may be in such a location if it is on a major road, abuts a commercial district, is adjacent to a police station, fire station, school, playground, or cemetery, if it is on the *wrong side of the tracks* of a particular town, or simply near the (train) tracks. However, for every five people who may think your home and its location is not for them, there is one who will think that it is great. For the person who has rented for several years in a three family urban setting with no trees and no backyard, a home with a small lot and a few trees next to a playground is *country living*. Focus your marketing in towns where your location would be considered a move-up.

Asking Price is Too High

Pricing your home is the single most important marketing decision you will make. When determining the price, the *for sale by owner seller* needs to be able to step back and evaluate the home objectively. Many have trouble doing this and price their homes too high. By the time they realize this and lower the price, the home has become *stale* and lost the freshness and excitement that a newly-listed home brings. If you believe you need to lower the price, lower it in small 1% to 2% increments ($4,000-$8,000 on a $400,000 home) every 10 to 14 days until you get some noticeable interest. If you instead drastically lower it all at once, you may go too far unnecessarily and cut into your proceeds.

PROACTIVE SELLING TIPS

Your home sale situation may not fit nicely into any of the four problem-categories. Or, it may fit in all four. However, if the earlier suggestions do not work, consider the following.

Offer Owner Financing

You will open up your market of potential buyers to those who cannot qualify for conventional financing if you offer *owner financing*. There will be some risk involved in owner financing. Carefully evaluate your buyer's credit worthiness and have your attorney assist you in preparing the documents, such as the mortgage and note. By doing this, you should be able to significantly reduce the risk and sell your home. (See Chapter 8 for more information.)

Use a Flat-Rate Broker Arrangement

One large drawback of selling by owner is the inability to have your home seen by brokers on the *MLS system* and by homebuyers via *Realtor.com*. However, as described in Chapter 5, by-owner websites now offer MLS exposure for an additional fee. As part of this choice, you will have to agree to pay a 2%–3% fee to the broker who brings the eventual buyer. However, 2%–3% is far better than paying 4%–7%.

Contact Local Brokers

To help supplement the above option, call several of the brokers in your area. Let them know you are trying to sell your home by yourself but have listed it on MLS and are quite willing to compensate them with a *finder's fee* of 2%–3%. You can then inform them that as soon as you sell, you will be searching for another home and would need an agent for assistance. This may encourage them to help find someone for you as it will may provide them with a *2 for 1* package. They will appreciate the call, and as a result of speaking to you personally, they will no longer be suspect of collecting their fee if they find you a buyer, and accordingly will be more comfortable showing your home to prospective buyers.

Even, if you choose to not list through MLS, call several agents anyway and let them know that you are eager to sell and that you are willing to pay a *buyer's broker's* commission of 2%–3%. Ordinarily, if a broker is assisting a buyer to find a home, the broker may intentionally skip over for sale by owner homes because of the risk that the seller will be difficult to deal with and not agree to pay the broker's commission. However, speaking with several agents will let them know that you are knowledgeable about and agreeable to the potential arrangement. In your advertisements, you can further publicize your feelings by including the phrase *buyer's brokers welcome*.

Consider an Alternative/Discount Broker

Some brokers and agencies have seen the trend is turning away from full-commission agencies. Over the last 10 years or so, they have started alternative and discount agencies that offer sellers varying degrees of service for less than full commission. Some agencies offer a *documents only* program for approximately $1,000 wherein the seller does the marketing and the agency provides and helps the seller complete the contract once the seller finds a buyer. Some agencies offer to market the home (without placing the home on MLS) under a *90-day exclusive right to sell agreement* (where the agency obtains a commission when the home sells regardless of whether they brought in the buyer) for approximately a 2% commission.

Other agencies will charge you a flat rate fee of approximately $5,000 to market your home and if one of their agents sells it, they will be entitled to another $5,000 or so. Look for these agencies in your area through the telephone directory under *real estate agencies* or on the Internet using *discount real estate agencies [your state]* as a search term. Also, review their advertising in newspapers and homes-for-sale magazines to observe their quality and to see how extensive it is.

SELECTING A FULL-COMMISSION BROKER

Hopefully, with the assistance of this book, you will be able to *close the deal* on your home yourself, or at least with a flat rate or discounted agent. However, it is inevitable that some will have more difficulty than others and will want to revert back to the more conventional approach of using a full commission broker. If you read through the book, utilized some of the recommendations, and gave it an honest effort, then there is no shame in doing so. The following suggestions may prove valuable when selecting an agent.

You want to select an agent (and agency) whose display advertisements blanket the area and provide great exposure to their seller-customers. It you easily can find a broker's advertisements out there, then hopefully your eventual buyer will find your home the same way. Some agents and brokers make a real commitment to advertising, while others are quite stingy about spending money on advertising. Investigate the various newspapers, local brokers' websites, and homes-for-sale publications to see who will invest advertising dollars on your behalf.

Ask for Personal Referrals

As you have seen throughout this book, an informed, personal referral is a great way to narrow your search. People who often work closely with real estate agents are real estate attorneys, title companies, bankers, mortgage lenders, and insurance agents are your best source for a referral. They will know which ones are hard workers, talented sales people, and sincere. Moreover, the agent will be more apt to treat you extra-well in order to please the referring party so as to *earn* additional referrals from him or her.

SELLING TIPS

Choose an agent who works and lives in your town or the immediate surrounding area.

Select a Local Agent

It is not uncommon to see sellers list their homes with agencies from outside their town and even outside the neighboring towns. Perhaps the agent is someone they know and feel obligated to use. Perhaps the agent was referred by a trusted friend or family member. Regardless of the reason, using an agent outside your town or area can be a significant mistake.

The agent likely works in an office that only advertises in certain newspapers and publications. If those newspapers and publications are circulated in a different geographic area, they probably will not hit your target market of prospective buyers. Moreover, an agent will not know the other agents in the area who will likely be showing your home. Therefore, your agent will not have a good working relationship with them.

Finally, your agent may not know any of the detailed facts about your town and therefore may not be ready to answer the common questions of a prospective buyer about it.

Choose a Full-Time Agent

Many agents work part-time or are semi-retired, but will not tell this to their potential customers. Some of these *part-timers* will work hard to obtain your listing, but then take it easy or will be busy working their other job, all the while hoping that someone else finds a buyer for you so that they can obtain their commission. Full-time agents count on their commissions as their sole employment income. For them, it is not a hobby or *extra* money.

Ask for a CMA

After you have obtained some names of potential agents, contact them and have them perform a *comparative market analysis* (CMA) on your home. When they have completed it, invite them to your home to discuss it as well as the price they would set for your home and their plan to market it. Beware of those that try to *buy your listing* by telling you that your home should sell for a price significantly higher than both what you believe it will sell for and what the other agents inform you. This is a common practice by unscrupulous agents who try to win you as a customer by making you think that it will sell for the high price only to later convince you to lower it once he or she *lands the listing*. Instead, you want someone who is not afraid to give you the realistic picture of how your home compares with other recent similar sales and what your sale prospects are.

Ask your agent how he or she plans to market your home. Observe how your agent presents him or herself when answering. You want someone who has put some thought into this *before* your meeting. You also want someone that comes across with confidence, knowledge, and grace. The impression made on you will likely be the same impression made on your prospective buyers.

Look at the physical CMA report that the agent hands to you. The CMA is a good test to see how adept your agent and his or her office is at putting together marketing materials. If their CMA makes a great presentation, then it is likely that their listing sheet, advertisements, and mailings will be at the same level.

Select the Person First and Salesperson Second

When you meet a prospective agent, he or she will be dealing with you much in the same way they will be dealing with your prospective buyer. Although, at this point, they will not be selling a home, they will be selling themselves. Do they come across too brazen and cocky such that it turns you off, or do they come across as a *down to earth* genuine and sincere person who is listening to you and your needs? Your agent will be dealing with your prospective buyers and other agents. Your home will appear that much more desirable if your prospective buyers feel comfortable with your agent. Arrogant or pushy salespeople annoy others and may taint the way your home is viewed.

You will want to detail and describe to your agent the many features about the home only a seller would know. Accordingly, you want an agent who is willing and eager to learn what you can tell them. This will only make their job of selling easier. Many agents unfortunately pretend to listen, but never make notes of a home's particulars and then never relay this to buyers when conducting a showing. After speaking with and interviewing a few brokers, you will have a sense of who is really listening and who is only pretending.

MAKE THE LISTING AGREEMENT IN YOUR BEST INTEREST

After you have met and spoken with several agent-candidates and have chosen one to list your home, you will now need to execute a *listing agreement*. The listing agreement is the contract that governs your relationship with your agent. It spells out each of your rights and obligations. Once this is signed, all of the promises, representations, and plans that your agent previously orally conveyed to you are meaningless. Therefore, it is important to carefully review the agreement to make sure it spells out what you want.

The listing agreement is a pre-written contract. The only blanks that your agent will need to fill in are likely:

◆ your name;
◆ the home's address;
◆ the agreed-upon listing price of the home;
◆ the percentage commission that the will be due the agent upon the sale;
◆ the listing period; and,
◆ the type of marketing you will authorize (a lawn sign, open houses, etc.).

Because it is pre-written, most sellers believe that it is a *standard* contract and do not realize that they can and should negotiate its terms; however, there are several *types* of listing agreements available to you.

Types of Listing Agreements

There are three types of listing agreements:the exclusive right to sell, the exclusive agency, and the open listing.

Exclusive Right to Sell

The *exclusive right to sell* is the most favorable to your agent. It states that the agent's commission is due if the property is sold during the term of the agreement *by anyone*. So, if after trying to sell your home by yourself for 6 months, you sign an exclusive right to sell listing agreement with your broker and on the next day someone who saw your home 2 weeks ago (before you had an agent) comes and makes and offer and eventually buys it, you will have to pay the agent the full commission.

Exclusive Agency

With an *exclusive agency agreement*, the commission is due to your agent if *any* real estate broker is the procuring cause of the sale during the term of the agreement. If the seller finds the buyer, then no commission is due.

Open Listing

The *open listing agreement* is the most favorable to the seller. A commission is due to the agent only if he or she is the first party to procure a ready, willing, and able buyer.

Negotiate Terms of the Agreement

The type of listing agreement varies on what part of the country you are in. If you are presented an *exclusive right to sell listing agreement*, you should always try to negotiate it into an *exclusive agency* or an *open listing*. The exclusive right to sell does not motivate your agent to work as hard for you as the other two types.

In requesting one of the other two types of listings, you may be met by opposition by the agency. It may be that you are in an area where the exclusive right to sell is so predominant that changing it is not negotiable. In this case, be sure to, at the very least, protect your prior hard work when you attempted to sell the home by yourself. Attach an addendum to the contract listing the names and addresses of each and every person who approached you as a result of your attempt to sell the home by yourself. The *sign-in sheets* from your open houses and showings will be the best source for these names. The following language can then be inserted in the listing agreement—

> *Agent hereby acknowledges that Seller has attempted to market the Premises by him/herself by owner during the period of _____ to _____ . During that period, the individuals identified in the attached Addendum were procured by Seller and were shown the Premises by Seller. Accordingly, Agent agrees that if any person listed on the said addendum purchases the Premises, Agent will not be due any commission whatsoever.*

The right agent will respect your prior efforts to sell the home yourself and will allow you to exempt those people who previously came to see the home.

Define the Terms

Your agreement will state that the agent is due a commission when your home sells. The agreement may further define what constitutes a *sale*. It may be that before the agent is due a commission, the closing has to occur, the seller needs to transfer the deed to the buyer, and the seller has to receive his or her proceeds check. However, it also may be stated that *all* the agent has to do is procure a *ready, willing,* and *able* buyer who signs a *Purchase and Sale Agreement*. If the deal falls apart after that, the agent is still entitled to a full commission. Also, if the buyer wrongfully breaches the agreement and the seller retains the deposit as his or her remedy, some agreements will allow the agent to retain part of the deposit as commission even though the home did not sell. Further, your agreement may require the agent to be paid his or her full commission if the reason why the closing was not accomplished was due to the fault of the seller.

Remember, you have hired your agent to do one thing—*sell your home*. A fee should not be paid unless this is done and you have received your proceeds. If the agent were to be entitled to a fee when the deal, for whatever reason, broke down after the *Purchase and Sale Agreement* was signed, you would have to pay this out of your pocket and not from the sale proceeds. This could cause you great financial harm. You should insist in the agreement that the agent be entitled to the commission—

> *if and only if the deed is accepted and recorded and the seller obtains the benefit of the full proceeds and not otherwise.*

Moreover, if the buyer wrongfully backs out of the deal, you should not share the forfeited deposit escrow with the agent. The deposit is to compensate you for the time and expenses lost as a result of the buyer's breach. The agent instead needs to go back to work and find a new buyer who will complete the deal.

SELLING TIPS

The listing agreement may, although not likely, be unclear or even silent as to when a commission is due. If it is, the majority of states' common law will allow the agent to be paid when the agent procures a ready, willing, and able buyer—even if the sale is not closed.

Also, if the seller refuses to sign a *Purchase and Sale Agreement* with a ready, willing, and able buyer whom the broker has procured, some states will require the seller to pay the agent the commission. To rectify this, limit the authority of the agent by changing *sole and exclusive right to sell* to *sole and exclusive right to solicit offers*. (Check with your attorney for the law in your particular state so that you can keep this in mind.)

Limit the Length of the Listing Agreement

Listing Agreements are valid for only the term specified in the agreement itself. Terms vary depending on area, but you can expect to have your agent request a 6-month agreement. If the agreement is an exclusive right to sell, then this means that if your home is sold, by anyone, anytime over the next six months, the agent will be due a commission. Technically, only a buyer needs to be procured within the six months and not the closing.

This is a real comfortable position for the broker to be in as it will be only on rare occasions where no buyer comes forward during the six months. It is a natural human tendency to procrastinate until a deadline date approaches. Consequently, the longer the term of the listing agreement, the less incentive there is for the agent to work hard to find a buyer. Some agents with 6-month terms, will only employ a real aggressive marketing plan in the fourth or fifth month when they sense they may lose the listing if a buyer is not found.

In order to induce the agent to market your home aggressively from the start of the arrangement, ask for a shorter term—say 90 days. You should explain to your agent that you cannot afford to wait 6 months. Explain that if he or she is performing well during the 90 days, but for whatever reason a buyer is not found, you will be loyal and renew the agreement. A good agent will be confident in his or her abilities to impress and satisfy you (whether or not a buyer is found) and should oblige.

Commission is Negotiable

When you are ready to sign the listing agreement, the agent already may have completed the commission rate without even discussing it with you. Do not be fooled into thinking that all agents' fees are set at a particular number say 5% or 6%. In fact, it is against the anti-trust laws for agencies to collude and set a certain fixed rate. The real estate business is extremely competitive, and now with the increase of owners selling by themselves, even more so. You will find agents open to negotiate their fee, especially during a seller's market, when homes are selling quickly and for top dollar. A fee of 4.5% or even 4% is common during such times.

Your agent may attempt to argue that at a lower fee, there will be less incentive for other agents to bring a buyer to see the home. This is not necessarily true. If a buyer's agent knows that his or her buyer is looking for a home of your style and in your area, it does not make sense that the agent intentionally avoid showing your home because he or she will make 2.0% instead of 2.5%. The faster the buyer's agent can find a home for his or her buyer, the faster he or she can wrap up the deal and move on to the next buyer. Further, if a buyer's agent is only looking for the best deal for him or herself and not for the buyer, he or she is not serving the customer and will not be very successful.

In any event, in response to your agent's contention, you can request that your agent split, for example a 4.5% commission by giving 2.5% to the buyer's agent and having your agent retain 2.0%. There is no requirement that the listing broker earn the same fee as the selling broker. Moreover, if there is to be a premium paid, it stands to reason that it should be on the agent finding the buyer and not the one merely listing the home.

Same agency discount

When your agent (and his or her office), in addition to listing your home, also finds the buyer, this is a windfall for them. They will make full commission and not have to share it with any other agency. Therefore, negotiate a discounted rate in your listing agreement to cover such a scenario. You should find that your agent will agree to reduce the commission to something between half of the commission and full commission. For example, if the agreed-upon commission is 5%, your agent (or his or her agency), if asked, may agree to a commission between 3% and 4% if that office also procures the buyer who buys your home.

Marketing Requirements

You may be surprised to learn that most listing agreements do not require a listing agent to perform any specific marketing tasks in attempt to sell your home. The number of times he or she advertises your home, the publications the advertisement are put in, whether or not flyers are sent out to the neighborhood, whether or not any open houses are held, and the number or frequency of the open houses are all subject to the agent's discretion and not strictly mandated by the pre-printed terms of the listing agreement. Moreover, it is not likely that your agent will voluntarily set a minimum requirement for marketing. Therefore, if you have certain requests and expectations as to how your agent will perform his or her job, you will need to negotiate these in the listing agreement.

There is a fine line between making sure that your agent gives enough attention and exposure to your home and micromanaging and second-guessing his or her efforts. Agents will not be happy (and may not accept) your directing the marketing campaign. Such decisions as how to word the advertising and in which publications the advertising should appear are best left to the discretion of your agent. However, you should impose minimum requirements as to how frequently the agent must advertise the home and also how frequently he or she should host an open house.

You may, for example, require that the home be advertised in the *customary fashion* in at least one newspaper or magazine publication each week and that there be at least two open houses per calendar month. Agents (and their offices) have a certain, limited advertising budget for their listings, and, by imposing these requirements, you will help to make sure that they do not overlook your home for others. This can be a real concern especially if your home is on the lower end of the price chain.

In order to enforce any minimum requirements that you negotiate, ask to have the listing agreement made contingent on your agent adhering to them. In other words, if your agent does not comply with the agreed-upon minimum requirements, you will have the right to void the listing agreement and retain another agent.

Whether you resolve to complete the sale of your home by yourself or you resort to utilizing the services of an agent, take comfort in knowing that there is a always a buyer for every home. During your pursuit of him or her, remember a few suggestions:

◆ know and anticipate your options;
◆ stay a step ahead of the process;
◆ ask the right questions of the right people;
◆ use your creativity; and,
◆ think objectively and with an open mind.

As the ancient Chinese proverb says, *the longest journey starts with a single step*. The marketing and sale of a home done for sale by owner *is* a long journey. Continue each day to take positive steps toward your goal, and you will be just fine.

Good luck, and happy home selling.

Glossary

A

appraiser (real estate). A state-licensed professional who is trained to evaluate homes and other real estate and determine what they are worth.

B

binder. *See offer.*

buyer's market. A term used to identify conditions that hinder the sale of homes and cause price concessions. These conditions may include a shortage of homebuyers, a large supply of homes for sale, high mortgage interest rates, and overall poor economic conditions.

buyer's agent. The real estate agent whose customer is the buyer and who, therefore, owes a fiduciary (high level) duty to the buyer. (Also referred to as *buyer's broker.*)

C

closing. The step of the home selling process where the buyer tenders the balance of the agreed-upon price and the seller signs over title to the home via the deed.

CMA (Comparative Market Analysis). The process by which a real estate agent or homeowner can compare the subject home with other recent sales to determine an approximate value. A CMA is not as scientific or precise as an appraisal done by a licensed appraiser.

contract to purchase. *See offer.*
county recorder's office. *See registry of deeds.*

D

deed. A written document that, when signed by the seller/owner, transfers ownership (title) to another (the buyer).

deed of trust. *See mortgage.*

default. Term used to describe when either the seller or buyer has violated the terms of the Purchase and Sale Agreement.

defects. A matter appearing in the chain of title and revealed by a title search that may prevent the seller from transferring clear record and marketable title.

deposit receipt. *See offer.*

directional signs. Small signs that supplement the main yard sign. They typically are set in the ground on the 2 or 3 roads leading to the home to promote an open house.

discharge. A document that is issued by a lender that confirms that a promissory note and the ancillary mortgage have been fully paid and satisfied. The discharge is recorded at the registry of deeds.

E

easement. A right of use over the property of another.

encumbrance. *See defect.*

escrow. The process in which the buyer's deposit is placed in the hands of a third person and held by that person until the closing is complete.

executory period. Period after the parties sign the Purchase and Sale Agreement, but before the closing.

F

fair market value. The price a willing buyer will agree to pay to a willing seller.

fair housing act. The federal statute that prohibits many forms of discrimination in the marketing, sale, or rental of housing.

for sale by owner (FSBO). It signifies a home that is being sold by its owner and not through a real estate agency.

G

gross living area (GLA). The square footage of the interior of a home.

L

liquidated damages. A provision in the Purchase and Sale Agreement that calls for the forfeiture of the deposit by the buyer to the seller when the buyer fails to fulfill his or her obligations under the Purchase and Sale Agreement.

listing agent. The agent who works for and owes a fiduciary duty to the seller.

listing sheet. A document commonly produced by a real estate agent or for sale by owner seller in the marketing of a home. It usually provides a photograph of the home and details many of the features of the home, including number and types of rooms, room sizes, lot size, mechanical system descriptions, and a remarks section.

M

mechanic's lien. A lien or encumbrance on the title to an owner's home that a contractor who performs work on the home can file at the registry of deeds (or office of the recorder) if the owner fails to pay for the services rendered.

MLS (multiple listing service). A nation-wide computer repository for all homes on the market that are listed with a real estate agent. (The MLS system is only accessible to real estate agents.)

mortgage. The name of the document signed by a borrower/buyer that grants an interest in the buyer's land and secures the buyer's performance of monies borrowed from the lender.

mortgage discharge. *See discharge.*

O

open house.   A marketing tool used in the home sale process wherein the owner (or agent) advertises that a home may be toured during a set time.

offer.   In states and areas that use two documents during the purchase process, this is the first, simpler document that the buyer completes, signs, and forwards to the seller. It contains the basic terms necessary for the sale.

P

plot plan.   A one-page diagram of the shape and dimensions of the lot showing where the home and other structures are located. The plot plan is drafted by a licensed land surveyor or civil engineer.

purchase and sale agreement.   The document that contains all of the rights and obligations governing the buyer's purchase and the seller's sale of a home.

purchase money mortgage.   Term referring to money lent to the buyer by the seller for the purposes of allowing the buyer to purchase the home. Typically used to refer to the seller's loan being the first mortgage.

Q

quitclaim deed.   A deed that passes on title to the buyer, but only to the extent of what the seller possessed. It does not guarantee that the title is clear.

R

realtor.   The title given to a real estate agent or broker who is also a member of the National Association of Realtors, the largest national industry organization for real estate agents.

recorder's office.   *See registry of deeds.*

registry of deeds.   The physical office or department where deeds, mortgages, and all matters affecting title to land in a particular district are recorded so as to provide notice to the public.

risk of loss.   Refers to the burden that one party bears of something happening to the home during the period after the parties sign the Purchase and Sale Agreement, but before the closing.

S

seller's market. A term used to identify conditions that allow for the quick sale of homes at top prices. These conditions may include a shortage of homes for sale, a large supply of buyers, low mortgage interest rates, and overall good economic conditions.

selling agent. The real estate agent who finds and procures the buyer for a seller's home. The selling agent may be a subagent for the seller, thereby owing his or her duty to the seller, or may be a buyer's agent, thereby owing his or her duty to the buyer.

settlement statement. A two page document required by the federal government that contains the full itemization of all of the seller's and buyer's credits and debits for the closing.

specific performance. The name of the remedy whereby a buyer requests a court order to force the seller to sell when the seller has failed to transfer title to the buyer, in violation of the terms of the Purchase and Sale Agreement.

subagent. Refers to the agent who finds and procures a buyer for a seller's property, but who is deemed to work for the benefit of the listing agent and the seller, and therefore owes a duty to the seller, not the buyer.

survey. *See plot plan.*

T

title. The status of ownership. For purposes of the Purchase and Sale Agreement, refers to the quality of ownership that the seller is required to pass to the buyer. It is standard for Purchase and Sale Agreements to call for the highest quality, by using the words clear record and marketable title.

title company. An organization whose principle function is to conduct real estate closings.

title defect. *See defect.*

title examination. The process by which records at the registry of deeds are reviewed to determine whether the title to a particular piece of real estate is good or whether there are defects.

W

warranty deed. A deed in which the seller guarantees that his or her ownership is free from defects.

Internet Resources

The following list of Internet resources should provide the *for sale by owner seller* assistance and guidance on several of the steps along the path to selling your own home.

Find Prices of Recent Sales in Your Area:
    www.domania.com
    www.fsboadvertisingservice.com/saleprices.asp

Online Comparative Market Analysis:
    www.homegain.com
    www.housevalues.com
    www.ourhomesprice.com
    www.priceahomeonline.com
    www.ushomevalue.com

For Sale By Owner Advertising Sites:
    www.2buyhomes.net
    www.byowner.com
    www.forsalebyowner.com
    www.fsboadvertising.com
    www.homesalez.com
    www.salebyownerrealty.com

National Association of Realtors:
www.realtor.com
(provides listings for all agent-listed homes in country)

Purchase and Sale Agreement Forms:
www.findlegalforms.com
www.uslegalforms.com

Seller-Financing Options:
www.myfico.com
(explains the FICO scoring system)
www.equifax.com
(national credit reporting agency)
www.experian.com
(national credit reporting agency)
www.transunion.com
(national credit reporting agency)
www.mortgage-calc.com
(mortgage calculator and other related features)

Index

About the Author

Joseph P. DiBlasi has been an attorney in private practice since 1992. In addition to his other practice areas, he regularly represents and counsels residential and commercial real estate sellers, buyers, developers, investors, lenders, landlords, and tenants.

A true believer in the popular expression, "(a)n ounce of prevention is worth a pound of cure," and knowing that individuals who seek legal help often do so *after* there has been irreparable damage, Attorney DiBlasi has written several self-help books to provide needed legal information to individuals at the very earliest stages.

He has been a guest speaker for various civic organizations and has been featured on television and radio programs as well as in newspaper articles. In addition to his law practice and his writing, he invests time and energy in real estate, enjoys traveling, fitness, politics, and reading non-fiction. He is an avid college hockey fan and is active in the local Chamber of Commerce, serving as the immediate past president.

He and his wife, Laura, a dressmaker, reside in Massachusetts with their new son, Dario.

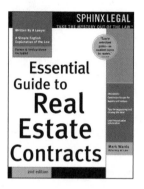

SPHINX® PUBLISHING'S NATIONAL TITLES
Valid in All 50 States

LEGAL SURVIVAL IN BUSINESS

The Complete Book of Corporate Forms	$24.95
The Complete Patent Book	$26.95
The Entrepreneur's Internet Handbook	$21.95
How to Form a Limited Liability Company (2E)	$24.95
Incorporate in Delaware from Any State	$24.95
Incorporate in Nevada from Any State	$24.95
How to Form a Nonprofit Corporation (2E)	$24.95
How to Form Your Own Corporation (4E)	$26.95
How to Form Your Own Partnership (2E)	$24.95
How to Register Your Own Copyright (4E)	$24.95
How to Register Your Own Trademark (3E)	$21.95
Most Valuable Business Legal Forms You'll Ever Need (3E)	$21.95
Profit from Intellectual Property	$28.95
Protect Your Patent	$24.95
The Small Business Owner's Guide to Bankruptcy	$21.95

LEGAL SURVIVAL IN COURT

Attorney Responsibilities & Client Rights	$19.95
Crime Victim's Guide to Justice (2E)	$21.95
Grandparents' Rights (3E)	$24.95
Help Your Lawyer Win Your Case (2E)	$14.95
Jurors' Rights (2E)	$12.95
Legal Research Made Easy (3E)	$21.95
Winning Your Personal Injury Claim (2E)	$24.95
Your Rights When You Owe Too Much	$16.95

LEGAL SURVIVAL IN REAL ESTATE

Essential Guide to Real Estate Contracts (2E)	$18.95
Essential Guide to Real Estate Leases	$18.95
How to Buy a Condominium or Townhome (2E)	$19.95
How to Buy Your First Home	$18.95
Working with Your Homeowners Association	$19.95

LEGAL SURVIVAL IN PERSONAL AFFAIRS

101 Complaint Letters That Get Results	$18.95
The 529 College Savings Plan	$16.95
The Antique and Art Collector's Legal Guide	$24.95
Cómo Hacer su Propio Testamento	$16.95
Cómo Restablecer su propio Crédito y Renegociar sus Deudas	$21.95
Cómo Solicitar su Propio Divorcio	$24.95
The Complete Kit to Selling Your Own Home	$18.95
The Complete Legal Guide to Senior Care	$21.95
Credit Smart	$18.95
Family Limited Partnership	$26.95
Gay & Lesbian Rights	$26.95
Guía de Inmigración a Estados Unidos (3E)	$24.95
Guía de Justicia para Víctimas del Crimen	$21.95
How to File Your Own Bankruptcy (5E)	$21.95
How to File Your Own Divorce (5E)	$26.95
How to Make Your Own Simple Will (3E)	$18.95
How to Write Your Own Living Will (3E)	$18.95
How to Write Your Own Premarital Agreement (3E)	$24.95
Inmigración a los EE. UU. Paso a Paso	$22.95
Living Trusts and Other Ways to Avoid Probate (3E)	$24.95
Manual de Beneficios para el Seguro Social	$18.95
Mastering the MBE	$16.95
Most Valuable Personal Legal Forms You'll Ever Need (2E)	$26.95
Neighbor v. Neighbor (2E)	$16.95
The Nanny and Domestic Help Legal Kit	$22.95
The Power of Attorney Handbook (4E)	$19.95
Repair Your Own Credit and Deal with Debt (2E)	$18.95
El Seguro Social Preguntas y Respuestas	$14.95
Sexual Harassment: Your Guide to Legal Action	$18.95
The Social Security Benefits Handbook (3E)	$18.95
Social Security Q&A	$12.95
Teen Rights	$22.95
Traveler's Rights	$21.95
Unmarried Parents' Rights (2E)	$19.95
U.S. Immigration and Citizenship Q&A	$16.95
U.S. Immigration Step by Step	$21.95
U.S.A. Immigration Guide (4E)	$24.95
The Visitation Handbook	$18.95
The Wills, Estate Planning and Trusts Legal Kit	&26.95
Win Your Unemployment Compensation Claim (2E)	$21.95
Your Right to Child Custody, Visitation and Support (2E)	$24.95

SPHINX® PUBLISHING ORDER FORM

Charge my: ☐ VISA   ☐ MasterCard   ☐ American Express   ☐ **Money Order or Personal Check**

Credit Card Number   **Expiration Date**

Qty	ISBN	Title	Retail	Qty	ISBN	Title	Retail
		SPHINX PUBLISHING NATIONAL TITLES			1-57248-165-X	Living Trusts and Other Ways to Avoid Probate (3E)	$24.95
	1-57248-363-6	101 Complaint Letters That Get Results	$18.95		1-57248-186-2	Manual de Beneficios para el Seguro Social	$18.95
	1-57248-238-9	The 529 College Savings Plan	$16.95		1-57248-220-6	Mastering the MBE	$16.95
	1-57248-349-0	The Antique and Art Collector's Legal Guide	$24.95		1-57248-167-6	Most Val. Business Legal Forms You'll Ever Need (3E)	$21.95
	1-57248-347-4	Attroney Responsibilities & Client Rights	$19.95				
	1-57248-148-X	Cómo Hacer su Propio Testamento	$16.95		1-57248-360-1	Most Val. Personal Legal Forms You'll Ever Need (2E)	$26.95
	1-57248-226-5	Cómo Restablecer su propio Crédito y Renegociar sus Deudas	$21.95		1-57248-098-X	The Nanny and Domestic Help Legal Kit	$22.95
	1-57248-147-1	Cómo Solicitar su Propio Divorcio	$24.95		1-57248-089-0	Neighbor v. Neighbor (2E)	$16.95
	1-57248-166-8	The Complete Book of Corporate Forms	$24.95		1-57248-169-2	The Power of Attorney Handbook (4E)	$19.95
	1-57248-353-9	The Complete Kit to Selling Your Own Home	$18.95		1-57248-332-6	Profit from Intellectual Property	$28.95
	1-57248-229-X	The Complete Legal Guide to Senior Care	$21.95		1-57248-329-6	Protect Your Patent	$24.95
	1-57248-201-X	The Complete Patent Book	$26.95		1-57248-344-X	Repair Your Own Credit and Deal with Debt (2E)	$18.95
	1-57248-369-5	Credit Smart	$18.95		1-57248-350-4	El Seguro Social Preguntas y Respuestas	$14.95
	1-57248-163-3	Crime Victim's Guide to Justice (2E)	$21.95		1-57248-217-6	Sexual Harassment: Your Guide to Legal Action	$18.95
	1-57248-251-6	The Entrepreneur's Internet Handbook	$21.95		1-57248-219-2	The Small Business Owner's Guide to Bankruptcy	$21.95
	1-57248-346-6	Essential Guide to Real Estate Contracts (2E)	$18.95		1-57248-168-4	The Social Security Benefits Handbook (3E)	$18.95
	1-57248-160-9	Essential Guide to Real Estate Leases	$18.95		1-57248-216-8	Social Security Q&A	$12.95
	1-57248-254-0	Family Limited Partnership	$26.95		1-57248-221-4	Teen Rlghts	$22.95
	1-57248-331-8	Gay & Lesbian Rights	$26.95		1-57248-335-0	Traveler's Rights	$21.95
	1-57248-139-0	Grandparents' Rights (3E)	$24.95		1-57248-236-2	Unmarried Parents' Rights (2E)	$19.95
	1-57248-188-9	Guía de Inmigración a Estados Unidos (3E)	$24.95		1-57248-362-8	U.S. Immigration and Citizenship Q&A	$16.95
	1-57248-187-0	Guía de Justicia para Víctimas del Crimen	$21.95		1-57248-218-4	U.S. Immigration Step by Step	$21.95
	1-57248-103-X	Help Your Lawyer Win Your Case (2E)	$14.95		1-57248-161-7	U.S.A. Immigration Guide (4E)	$24.95
	1-57248-164-1	How to Buy a Condominium or Townhome (2E)	$19.95		1-57248-192-7	The Visitation Handbook	$18.95
	1-57248-328-8	How to Buy Your First Home	$18.95		1-57248-225-7	Win Your Unemployment Compensation Claim (2E)	$21.95
	1-57248-191-9	How to File Your Own Bankruptcy (5E)	$21.95				
	1-57248-343-1	How to File Your Own Divorce (5E)	$26.95		1-57248-330-X	The Wills, Estate Planning and Trusts Legal Kit	&26.95
	1-57248-222-2	How to Form a Limited Liability Company (2E)	$24.95		1-57248-138-2	Winning Your Personal Injury Claim (2E)	$24.95
	1-57248-231-1	How to Form a Nonprofit Corporation (2E)	$24.95		1-57248-333-4	Working with Your Homeowners Association	$19.95
	1-57248-345-8	How to Form Your Own Corporation (4E)	$26.95		1-57248-162-5	Your Right to Child Custody, Visitation and Support (2E)	$24.95
	1-57248-224-9	How to Form Your Own Partnership (2E)	$24.95				
	1-57248-232-X	How to Make Your Own Simple Will (3E)	$18.95		1-57248-157-9	Your Rights When You Owe Too Much	$16.95
	1-57248-200-1	How to Register Your Own Copyright (4E)	$24.95			**CALIFORNIA TITLES**	
	1-57248-104-8	How to Register Your Own Trademark (3E)	$21.95		1-57248-150-1	CA Power of Attorney Handbook (2E)	$18.95
	1-57248-233-8	How to Write Your Own Living Will (3E)	$18.95		1-57248-337-7	How to File for Divorce in CA (4E)	$26.95
	1-57248-156-0	How to Write Your Own Premarital Agreement (3E)	$24.95		1-57248-145-5	How to Probate and Settle an Estate in CA	$26.95
					1-57248-336-9	How to Start a Business in CA (2E)	$21.95
	1-57248-230-3	Incorporate in Delaware from Any State	$24.95		1-57248-194-3	How to Win in Small Claims Court in CA (2E)	$18.95
	1-57248-158-7	Incorporate in Nevada from Any State	$24.95		1-57248-246-X	Make Your Own CA Will	$18.95
	1-57248-250-8	Inmigración a los EE.UU. Paso a Paso	$22.95		1-57248-196-X	The Landlord's Legal Guide in CA	$24.95
	1-57071-333-2	Jurors' Rights (2E)	$12.95		1-57248-241-9	Tenants' Rights in CA	$21.95
	1-57248-223-0	Legal Research Made Easy (3E)	$21.95				

Form Continued on Following Page   **SubTotal** _____

Qty	ISBN	Title	Retail
		FLORIDA TITLES	
_____	1-57071-363-4	Florida Power of Attorney Handbook (2E)	$16.95
_____	1-57248-176-5	How to File for Divorce in FL (7E)	$26.95
_____	1-57248-356-3	How to Form a Corporation in FL (6E)	$24.95
_____	1-57248-203-6	How to Form a Limited Liability Co. in FL (2E)	$24.95
_____	1-57071-401-0	How to Form a Partnership in FL	$22.95
_____	1-57248-113-7	How to Make a FL Will (6E)	$16.95
_____	1-57248-088-2	How to Modify Your FL Divorce Judgment (4E)	$24.95
_____	1-57248-354-7	How to Probate and Settle an Estate in FL (5E)	$26.95
_____	1-57248-339-3	How to Start a Business in FL (7E)	$21.95
_____	1-57248-204-4	How to Win in Small Claims Court in FL (7E)	$18.95
_____	1-57248-202-8	Land Trusts in Florida (6E)	$29.95
_____	1-57248-338-5	Landlords' Rights and Duties in FL (9E)	$22.95
		GEORGIA TITLES	
_____	1-57248-340-7	How to File for Divorce in GA (5E)	$21.95
_____	1-57248-180-3	How to Make a GA Will (4E)	$21.95
_____	1-57248-341-5	How to Start a Business in Georgia (3E)	$21.95
		ILLINOIS TITLES	
_____	1-57248-244-3	Child Custody, Visitation, and Support in IL	$24.95
_____	1-57248-206-0	How to File for Divorce in IL (3E)	$24.95
_____	1-57248-170-6	How to Make an IL Will (3E)	$16.95
_____	1-57248-247-8	How to Start a Business in IL (3E)	$21.95
_____	1-57248-252-4	The Landlord's Legal Guide in IL	$24.95
		MARYLAND, VIRGINIA AND THE DISTRICT OF COLUMBIA	
_____	1-57248-240-0	How to File for Divorce in MD, VA and DC	$28.95
_____	1-57248-359-8	How to Start a Business in MD, VA or DC	$21.95
		MASSACHUSETTS TITLES	
_____	1-57248-128-5	How to File for Divorce in MA (3E)	$24.95
_____	1-57248-115-3	How to Form a Corporation in MA	$24.95
_____	1-57248-108-0	How to Make a MA Will (2E)	$16.95
_____	1-57248-248-6	How to Start a Business in MA (3E)	$21.95
_____	1-57248-209-5	The Landlord's Legal Guide in MA	$24.95
		MICHIGAN TITLES	
_____	1-57248-215-X	How to File for Divorce in MI (3E)	$24.95
_____	1-57248-182-X	How to Make a MI Will (3E)	$16.95
_____	1-57248-183-8	How to Start a Business in MI (3E)	$18.95
		MINNESOTA TITLES	
_____	1-57248-142-0	How to File for Divorce in MN	$21.95
_____	1-57248-179-X	How to Form a Corporation in MN	$24.95
_____	1-57248-178-1	How to Make a MN Will (2E)	$16.95
		NEW JERSEY TITLES	
_____	1-57248-239-7	How to File for Divorce in NJ	$24.95
		NEW YORK TITLES	
_____	1-57248-193-5	Child Custody, Visitation and Support in NY	$26.95
_____	1-57248-351-2	File for Divorce in NY	$26.95
_____	1-57248-249-4	How to Form a Corporation in NY (2E)	$24.95
_____	1-57248-095-5	How to Make a NY Will (2E)	$16.95
_____	1-57248-199-4	How to Start a Business in NY (2E)	$18.95
_____	1-57248-198-6	How to Win in Small Claims Court in NY (2E)	$18.95
_____	1-57248-197-8	Landlords' Legal Guide in NY	$24.95
_____	1-57071-188-7	New York Power of Attorney Handbook	$19.95
_____	1-57248-122-6	Tenants' Rights in NY	$21.95
		NORTH CAROLINA TITLES	
_____	1-57248-185-4	How to File for Divorce in NC (3E)	$22.95
_____	1-57248-129-3	How to Make a NC Will (3E)	$16.95
_____	1-57248-184-6	How to Start a Business in NC (3E)	$18.95
_____	1-57248-091-2	Landlords' Rights & Duties in NC	$21.95
		OHIO TITLES	
_____	1-57248-190-0	How to File for Divorce in OH (2E)	$24.95
_____	1-57248-174-9	How to Form a Corporation in OH	$24.95
_____	1-57248-173-0	How to Make an OH Will	$16.95
		PENNSYLVANIA TITLES	
_____	1-57248-242-7	Child Custody, Visitation and Support in PA	$26.95
_____	1-57248-211-7	How to File for Divorce in PA (3E)	$26.95
_____	1-57248-358-X	How to Form a Croporation in PA	$24.95
_____	1-57248-094-7	How to Make a PA Will (2E)	$16.95
_____	1-57248-357-1	How to Start a Business in PA (3E)	$21.95
_____	1-57248-245-1	The Landlord's Legal Guide in PA	$24.95
		TEXAS TITLES	
_____	1-57248-171-4	Child Custody, Visitation, and Support in TX	$22.95
_____	1-57248-172-2	How to File for Divorce in TX (3E)	$24.95
_____	1-57248-114-5	How to Form a Corporation in TX (2E)	$24.95
_____	1-57248-255-9	How to Make a TX Will (3E)	$16.95
_____	1-57248-214-1	How to Probate and Settle an Estate in TX (3E)	$26.95
_____	1-57248-228-2	How to Start a Business in TX (3E)	$18.95
_____	1-57248-111-0	How to Win in Small Claims Court in TX (2E)	$16.95
_____	1-57248-355-5	the Landlord's Legal Guide in TX	$24.95

SubTotal This page _____

SubTotal previous page _____

Shipping — $5.00 for 1st book, $1.00 each additional _____

Illinois residents add 6.75% sales tax _____

Connecticut residents add 6.00% sales tax _____

Total _____